Participa

Stories

15 Delightful Tales
that Promote the Development of
Oral Language, Listening, and Early Literacy Skills

by
Sherrill B. Flora

illustrated by
Vanessa Countryman

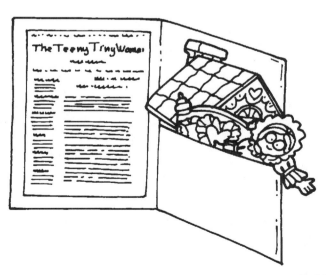

Publisher
Key Education Publishing Company LLC
Minneapolis, Minnesota

CONGRATULATIONS ON YOUR PURCHASE OF A KEY EDUCATION PRODUCT!

The editors at Key Education are former teachers who bring experience, enthusiasm, and quality to each and every product. Thousands of teachers have looked to the staff at Key Education for new and innovative resources to make their work more enjoyable and rewarding. Key Education is committed to developing and publishing educational materials that will assist teachers in building a strong and developmentally appropriate curriculum for young children.

PLAN FOR GREAT TEACHING EXPERIENCES WHEN YOU USE EDUCATIONAL MATERIALS FROM KEY EDUCATION PUBLISHING COMPANY, LLC

Credits
Author: Sherrill B. Flora
Creative Director: Annette Hollister-Papp
Cover Art: Annette Hollister-Papp
Inside Illustrations: Vanessa Countryman
Editor: George C. Flora
Production: Key Education Staff
Cover Photographs Credits:
   © Comstock, © Shutterstock

Key Education welcomes manuscripts and product ideas from teachers. For a copy of our submission guidelines, please send a self-addressed, stamped envelope to:

Key Education Publishing Company, LLC
Acquisitions Department
9601 Newton Avenue South
Minneapolis, Minnesota 55431

Standard Book Number: 1-933052-36-8
Participation Stories
Copyright © 2007 by Key Education Publishing Company, LLC
Minneapolis, Minnesota 55431

Table of Contents

Introduction

The fifteen rewritten tales found in *Participation Stories* are a delightful combination of traditional tales, folk tales, original tales, tales from other countries, and tales in rhyme. The stories and activity ideas will improve language skills, listening skills, and stimulate a love of words and reading in young children.

The following stories can be told, and retold, using all of the following techniques:

1. Traditional Storytelling (Auditory)

The first storytelling technique is for the teacher to become a traditional storyteller. Using this method, the teacher would simply tell the tale without the use of any text and the children would become an audience of eager listeners. Traditional storytellers must understand the content of their stories and be incredibly comfortable telling the tale. The teacher will need to spend a good deal of time practicing it before presenting the story to a group of children.

Once the teacher feels secure with the story content, gather the children together and bring the story to life by simply using your own words, facial expressions, gestures, and by utilizing a variety of voice inflections. Your audience will not only be captivated, but they will also be busy creating mental images as they listen to the words of the story.

Research has shown that this is a powerful tool for increasing language skills, listening skills, and for motivating young children to want to learn how to read and write.

2. Participation (or Action) Stories (Auditory and Kinesthetic)

The second technique for telling these stories is to turn them into participation or action stories. There are two different ways in which the children can participate — with **physical movements**, such as pantomiming the action words, or by **oral participation** as the children recite choral chants or repetitive phrases.

Physical Movements/Pantomime: Young children love being able to listen and move all at the same time. Each story has a variety of action words or phrases that are printed in **bold-italized** type. As the teacher reads the story, she should emphasize these words by slowing down each time she comes to a **bold-italized** word or phrase. This will signal the children to listen more carefully and to pantomime the actions. For example, "The bear was **sleeping** in his cave." The children would then pantomime that they are sleeping.

Some of the **bold-italized** words or phrases encourage the children to make various facial expressions, such as, "Then the little mouse **looked** at the duck." The children might squint or hold a hand over their eyes and pretend to be looking. This storytelling technique is an effective tool for building receptive language skills and for increasing vocabulary.

Oral Participation: In several of the stories there are **bold-italized** phrases that allow the children to orally participate. The children will learn a repetitive phrase or rhyme and will repeat it as a group each time a specific story clue for that phrase is read by the teacher. For example, in the tale, *Why the Bear is Stumpty-Tailed,* each time the teacher pauses and points, the children recite together, ***"The longest and bushiest and most beautiful tail in the forest."*** These are fun extra touches that can help the children learn basic concepts, increase language, and develop early literacy skills.

3. Prop Stories (Visual)

The third technique for telling these stories is to turn them into visual presentations. For hundreds of years storytellers have used visual techniques to enhance their tales. Hans Christian Andersen would create cut-out silhouettes of his story characters and use them like puppets. In China, the storyteller would bring visual movement to the stories by using hand shadows to create animated characters. In Japan, they made Kamishibai cards which are small paintings used to represent scenes from the story. Today, the storyteller is the classroom teacher who brings language and literature to life through words, print, and visual images, such as using story puppets or creating flannel board or magnetic board presentations.

All of the tales included in *Participation Stories* come with reproducible patterns that can be turned into puppets *(stick puppets or simple string puppets)*, as well as props for the flannel board or magnetic board. Use the following directions to turn the patterns from this book into a variety of visual storytelling aids.

Stick Puppets: Copy, color, cut out the patterns, and laminate them for durability. Attach each pattern to a craft stick or tongue depressor using double-sided tape. To create larger stick puppets, simply enlarge the patterns on a photocopy machine and finish as directed above. Attach these laminated patterns to paint stir sticks, 12-inch rulers, or wooden spoons.

String Puppets: Copy, color, cut out the patterns, and laminate them for durability. Fold a 3" x 5" index card in half lengthwise. Place a 24" piece of yarn or string along the fold and tape the card closed. Tape the two ends of the string to the back top of the pattern. The card is now a handle that the children can use to manipulate the string puppet. These string puppets have nice movement and are easy for small hands to manipulate.

Flannel Board or Magnetic Board Patterns: Copy, color, cut out the patterns, and laminate them for durability. For use on a flannel board, glue sandpaper or felt to the back of each pattern piece, or use self-stick Velcro®. For use on a magnetic board, attach a small piece of self-stick magnetic tape *(found at most craft or hardware stores)* on the back of each pattern.

Story Folders: Store the contents for each story in a pocket folder, or create your own pocket folder by stapling a 5.5" x 8.5" piece of card stock to the inside of a file folder. Pattern pieces can also be stored in a self-sealing plastic bag that is taped to the inside of the file folder. Attach the story to the left side of the folder and store the characters and/or scenery patterns in the pocket or bag on the right side of the folder *(see illustration)*.

Make Your Own Flannel Board: Foam board can be purchased at most craft or school supply stores. Cover the foam board with black felt by using glue *(only around the edges)* or wide double-sided tape. These flannel boards are lightweight for the children to use and are inexpensive to create. As an alternative for black felt, create a flannel board scene by using light blue felt for the sky, green felt for the grass, white felt for the clouds, and a yellow felt circle for the sun.

The Teeny Tiny Woman

– a traditional tale

This Story:

This is a fun story that is just a "teeny tiny" bit scary, which makes it particularly fun to use during the month of October. This story can be enjoyed anytime.

Basic Concepts:

1. Big and Little Concepts: Discuss the concepts of **big** and **little**. Explain that the words "teeny tiny" describe things that are very little. Provide the children with opportunities to explore objects that are big and small.

2. Open and Closed and In and Out Concepts: Copy the door pattern found on page 56 and use it for the Teeny Tiny Woman's cupboard in this story. Color it, cut it out, and then fold along the dotted line. Glue the door edge onto a piece of white paper so the door can be opened and closed. Draw and cut out a small bone. Use the cupboard door and the bone during the story. Also use these pieces to demonstrate the concepts of open and closed (**open** and **close** the door), and in and out (put the bone **in** the cupboard and take it **out** of the cupboard).

3. Vocabulary: Read the story in advance to identify the vocabulary that may be unfamiliar to your students,

The Teeny Tiny Woman

Once upon a time there was a teeny tiny woman *(fig. 1)*, who lived in a teeny tiny house *(fig. 2)*, in a teeny tiny town. One day, the teeny tiny woman **opened** her teeny tiny door and **walked** down her teeny tiny sidewalk *(fig. 5)*. She **pushed open** the teeny tiny gate *(fig. 4)* and began her teeny tiny **walk** to the teeny tiny town.

Once she reached the teeny tiny town, she **stopped** and **looked around** for the teeny tiny market. She found the teeny tiny market and **quickly walked** inside. Inside the teeny tiny market she saw a teeny tiny bone *(fig. 6)*. She **picked up** the teeny tiny bone and **carried it** over to the teeny tiny cashier. The teeny tiny woman **put** her teeny tiny **hand** in her teeny tiny pocket, **pulled out** her teeny tiny money and paid for the teeny tiny bone. She **put** the teeny tiny bone in a teeny tiny bag and **walked out of** the teeny tiny market. The teeny tiny woman **skipped** all the way back to her teeny tiny house.

The teeny tiny woman wanted to make a tasty teeny tiny soup with the teeny tiny bone. But she was a teeny tiny bit **tired**. She **yawned** a teeny tiny **yawn** and decided she needed a teeny tiny **nap**. So, the teeny tiny woman **opened** the teeny tiny door of her teeny tiny cupboard, *(See page 56.)* **put** the teeny tiny bone on the teeny tiny shelf, and then **closed** the teeny tiny cupboard door.

such as: **shivered, trembled,** and **shook.** Have the children practice pantomiming these actions before you read the story.

4. Predicting: The story never answers the question of "who or what" was saying, "Give me my bone!" Make a list of "who" the children think was talking. Also discuss if the bone ever was taken.

Pantomime/Act-it-Out Story Directions:

1. Pantomime: Read the **bold-italized** action words slowly. This will help the children to listen and know when and what to pantomime.

Read the story twice. First, let the girls pantomime the actions of the teeny tiny woman. Then read the story again and replace the words "woman, she, and her" with "man, he and his." The boys will enjoy pantomiming the story as *The Teeny Tiny Man.*

2. Say "Teeny Tiny": Another fun way to present the story is to teach the children the phrase, "**teeny tiny.**" Explain that each time you point or raise your hand the children should say "teeny tiny."

Flannel Board/Puppet Story Directions:

1. Visual Presentation: Follow the directions on page 5 to turn The *Teeny Tiny Woman* patterns (pages 8–9) into flannel board pieces or stick and string puppets.

2. Retell: Let the children manipulate the flannel board pieces or the puppets as you read the story. The children will also enjoy taking turns retelling the story all by themselves.

Then the teeny tiny woman **walked up** her teeny tiny stairs and **climbed into** her teeny tiny bed *(fig. 3)*. She **laid down** and **put** her teeny tiny head on her teeny tiny pillow, **closed her** teeny tiny eyes, and **fell asleep**.

The teeny tiny woman had only been asleep for a teeny tiny time, when suddenly she **jumped up!** She heard a big voice coming from the teeny tiny cupboard saying, "Give me my bone!" This made the teeny tiny woman a teeny tiny bit **scared**. She **shivered** teeny tiny **shivers**, **picked up** her teeny tiny blanket, and **covered** her teeny tiny head.

The teeny tiny woman **fell back asleep** but only for a teeny tiny time. Again, she heard the big voice coming from her teeny tiny cupboard saying, "Give me my bone!" The teeny tiny woman **sat up** in bed, **put** her teeny tiny hands **over** her teeny tiny ears, **laid back down**, and tried to get a teeny tiny bit more **sleep**.

The teeny tiny woman was still a teeny tiny bit **scared**. She **trembled** teeny tiny **trembles** and **shivered** teeny tiny **shivers** and **shook** teeny tiny **shakes**. Once again, the teeny tiny woman heard the big voice coming from her teeny tiny cupboard saying, "Give me my bone!"

But this time the teeny tiny woman became a teeny tiny bit **brave**. She **jumped out** of bed, **walked** on teeny tiny tip-toes, over to her teeny tiny bedroom door, and then yelled in her loudest teeny tiny voice, ***"Take it!"***

The End

The Teeny Tiny Woman Patterns

teeny tiny woman's house

(fig. 2)

teeny tiny woman

(fig. 1)

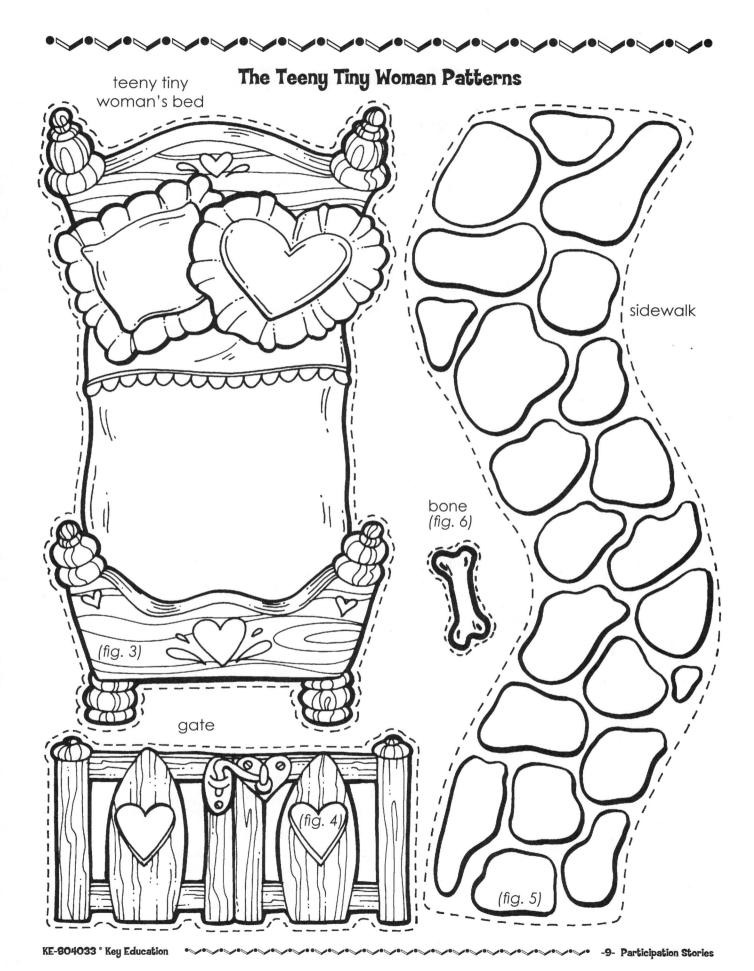

The Teeny Tiny Woman Patterns

teeny tiny woman's bed

sidewalk

bone (fig. 6)

(fig. 3)

gate

(fig. 4)

(fig. 5)

The Big, Big Turnip

- a traditional tale

This Story:

The story, *The Big, Big Turnip* can be enjoyed anytime, but it is especially fun during farm and gardening thematic units.

Basic Concepts:

1. Sequencing: This is an excellent story for developing sequencing skills. The story characters can be sequenced according to when they came to help pull out the turnip. The characters can also be sequenced according to size *(from largest to smallest or smallest to largest)*.

2. Vocabulary: Read the story in advance to identify the vocabulary that may be unfamiliar to your students. Many young children have never heard of, or tasted a turnip. Bring in a turnip to show the children. Let the children smell and taste the turnip. Draw a bar graph. Record the number of children who liked or disliked the turnip. Also graph how many children had previously tasted a turnip and how many children had never tasted one.

3. Drawing conclusions: Discuss whether or not the mouse really did help pull out the turnip. Did the first five characters loosen the turnip so they could have pulled it out without the mouse, or did the mouse add just enough extra strength that made the difference in pulling the turnip out of the ground?

The Big, Big Turnip

Once upon a time there was a farmer *(fig. 1)* who **dug** a small hole and **planted** a turnip seed. The farmer **watered** the seed and **waited** for it to grow. Before long the farmer saw that the turnip was ready to be **pulled out** of the ground. *(Add fig. 7. See flannel board directions #2 on Hide the Turnip, page 11)*

So, the farmer **bent over, grabbed** the top of the turnip, and **pulled** and **pulled** and **pulled** and **pulled**. As hard as the farmer tried, the turnip would not come out. So, the farmer **called** his wife who was busy **cooking** dinner.

> **Fe, fi, fo — fiddly-fum**
> **I *pulled* and *pulled* and *pulled* and *pulled*.**
> **Out — the turnip wouldn't come.**

The farmer's wife *(fig. 2)* came **running**. The farmer was **holding** onto the turnip, the wife **grabbed a hold** of the farmer, and the two of them **pulled** and **pulled** and **pulled** and **pulled**. As hard as they tried, the turnip would not come out. So, the farmer's wife **called** their daughter who was nearby **feeding** the dog.

> **Fe, fi, fo — fiddly-fum**
> **We *pulled* and *pulled* and *pulled* and *pulled*.**
> **Out — the turnip wouldn't come.**

The daughter *(fig. 3)* came **running**. The farmer was **holding** onto the turnip, the wife **was holding** onto the farmer, so the daughter **grabbed** a hold of the farmer's wife, and the three of them **pulled** and **pulled** and **pulled** and **pulled**. As hard as they tried, the turnip would not come out. So, the daughter **called** their dog who was busy **chasing** the cat.

> **Fe, fi, fo — fiddly-fum**
> **We *pulled* and *pulled* and *pulled* and *pulled*.**
> **Out — the turnip wouldn't come.**

Pantomime/Act-it-Out Story Directions:

1. Pantomime: Read the ***bold-italized*** action words slowly. This will help the children to listen and know when and what to pantomime.

Divide the children into groups of six and assign each child a character: farmer, farmer's wife, daughter, dog, cat, or mouse. The children will pantomime the actions of their character as the teacher reads the story.

2. Chant the Rhyme: Teach the children the repeated boxed "fe, fi, fo" 3-line rhyme, and then write the words on chart paper or poster board. The children will enjoy chanting the rhyme during the story.

Have the children cup their hands around their mouths when they recite the rhyme.

Flannel Board/Puppet Story Directions:

1. Visual Presentation: Follow the directions on page 5 to turn *The Big, Big Turnip* patterns (pages 12–13) into flannel board pieces or stick or string puppets.

2. Hide the Turnip: Use a piece of black or brown felt as the ground. Place the turnip behind the felt with only the green leaves showing. At the end of the story the turnip can really be pulled out of the ground.

3. Retell: Let the children manipulate the flannel board pieces or the puppets as you read the story. The children will also enjoy taking turns retelling the story all by themselves.

The dog *(fig. 4)* came ***running***. The farmer was ***holding*** the turnip, the wife was ***holding*** the farmer, the daughter was ***holding*** the farmer's wife, so the dog ***grabbed*** a hold of the daughter, and the four of them ***pulled*** and ***pulled*** and ***pulled*** and ***pulled***. As hard as they tried, the turnip would not come out. So, the dog ***called*** their cat who was busy ***chasing*** the mouse.

> **Fe, fi, fo — fiddly-fum**
> **We *pulled* and *pulled* and *pulled and pulled*.**
> **Out — the turnip wouldn't come.**

The cat *(fig. 5)* came ***running***. The farmer was ***holding*** the turnip, the wife was ***holding*** the farmer, the daughter was ***holding*** the farmer's wife, the dog was ***holding*** the daughter, so the cat ***grabbed*** a hold of the dog, and the five of them ***pulled*** and ***pulled*** and ***pulled*** and ***pulled***. As hard as they tried, the turnip would not come out. So, the cat ***called*** a mouse who was busy ***eating*** some cheese.

> **Fe, fi, fo — fiddly-fum**
> **We *pulled* and *pulled* and *pulled and pulled*.**
> **Out — the turnip wouldn't come.**

The mouse *(fig. 6)* came ***running***. The farmer, the farmer's wife, the daughter, dog, and the cat all said, "That mouse is far too little to help us."

The mouse squeaked a big squeak and said, "I could ***pull*** that turnip out of the ground all by myself, but since all of you have been pulling, I will ***grab*** the cat and help you.

The mouse ***grabbed*** a hold of the cat. The cat ***grabbed*** a hold of the dog. The dog ***grabbed*** a hold of the daughter. The daughter ***grabbed*** a hold of the farmer's wife. The farmer's wife ***grabbed*** a hold of the farmer, the farmer ***grabbed*** a hold of the turnip, and the six of them ***pulled*** and ***pulled*** and ***pulled*** and ***pulled***. And . . .

> **Fe, fi, fo — fiddly-fum**
> **We *pulled* and *pulled* and *pulled and pulled*.**
> **And out — the turnip did come!**

And the little mouse said, "I told you so."

THE END

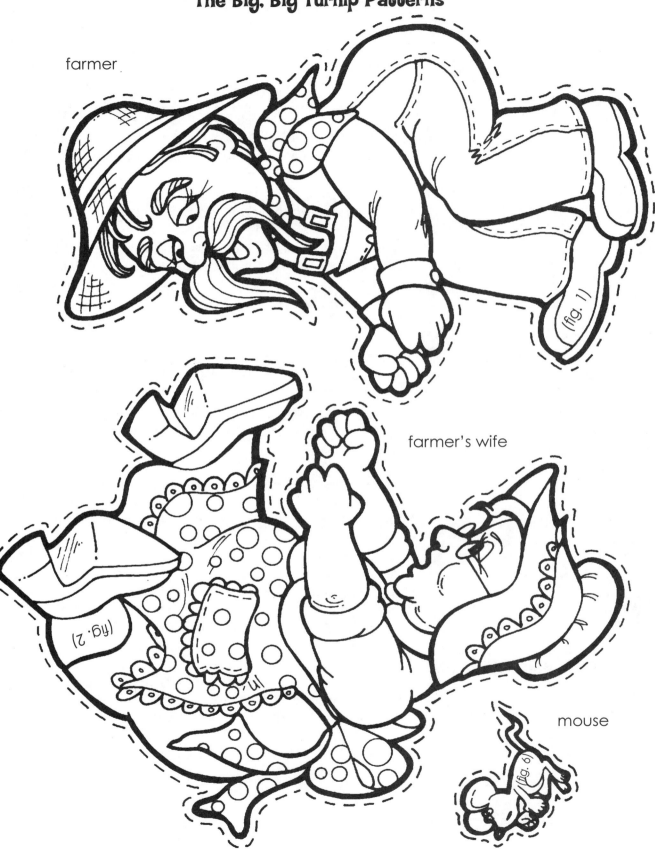

farmer

farmer's wife

mouse

(fig. 1)

(fig. 2)

(fig. 6)

The Big, Big Turnip Patterns

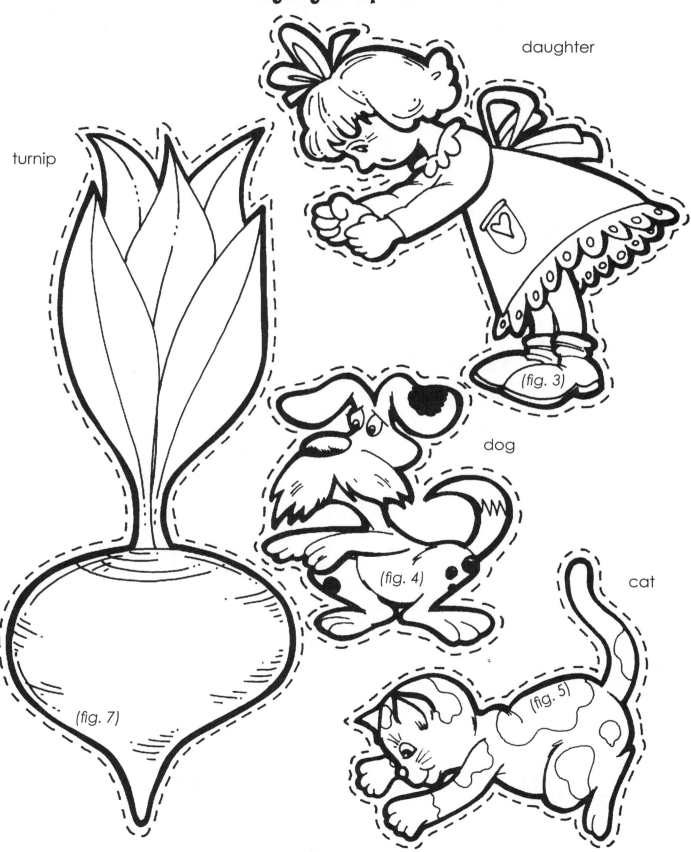

daughter

turnip

(fig. 3)

dog

(fig. 4)

cat

(fig. 5)

(fig. 7)

The Elephant and the Monkey

– a tale from India

This Story:

The story, *The Elephant and the Monkey* is a fable from India. It can be enjoyed anytime, but it is especially fun during farm and gardening thematic units.

Basic Concepts:

1. Opposites: Here is a list of some of the opposites that can be taught using this story: **big/little, fast/slow, tall/short, up/down, strong/weak, near/far,** and **long/short.** Some of these concepts are inferred in the story, so the teacher will have to point them out. For example, when the elephant and the monkey are looking at the trees across the river, the trees are **far away.** They are **near** the trees after they have crossed the river. Ask the children to give examples of the above concepts and then use the words in sentences.

2. Vocabulary: Read the story in advance to identify the vocabulary that may be unfamiliar to your students. Some new words may be: **argument, stretched, squeal, prance, wisest,** and **scampered.**

3. Compare and Contrast Venn Diagram: Draw a Venn diagram. One circle is for the qualities of the elephant, one circle is for the qualities of the monkey, and the overlapping section is for the qualities that are shared by both animals

The Elephant and the Monkey

Once upon a time there was a very big and very strong elephant *(fig. 1)* who spent a great deal of time arguing with a very little, yet very fast-moving monkey *(fig. 2)*.

The elephant would **prance** around and say, "Just look at how big and strong I am. I can **pull down** a tree using just my trunk." The elephant would then **swing his trunk**, **stamp** his feet, and say, "<u>**It is the best to be big and strong**</u>!"

The little monkey would **jump up and down** and squeal, "I can climb trees. I can swing by my tail." Then the monkey would **run** over to a tree, **climb up**, **swing** by his tail, and then **climb** back down the tree. The monkey would brag, "<u>**It is the best to be little and fast.**</u>"

The two animals had this argument everyday, so one day they decided that the argument had to come to an end. They had to know which one of them was really the best! The elephant said, "<u>**It is the best to be big and strong**</u>!" The monkey said, "<u>**It is the best to be little and fast.**</u>" The big elephant and the little monkey **walked** to the home of the owl—who was the wisest animal in the jungle.

The big elephant and the little monkey found the tree *(tree pattern, page 25)* where the wise owl *(fig. 3)* lived. They **sat down** on the ground and called up to him, "Please wise owl, **fly down** here and tell us which one of us is the best. Is it best to be big and strong or is it best to be little and fast?"

The wise owl said to them, "Do as I ask of you and you will discover which of you is the best. **Look over there**. Do you see the beautiful fruit trees on the other side of the river (such as, they both listened to the owl, they both wanted to get the fruit, and they both worked together.

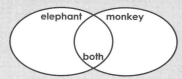

Pantomime/Act-it-Out Story Directions:

1. Pantomime: Read the **bold-italized** action words slowly. This will help the children to listen and know when and what to pantomime. Let the children decide if they want to pantomime the actions of the elephant or the monkey as the teacher reads the story.

2. Elephant and Monkey Chants: Teach the children the lines for the elephant and the monkey; The elephant said, "**It is the best to be big and strong**!" The monkey said, "**It is the best to be little and fast.**"

Flannel Board/Puppet Story Directions:

1. Visual Presentation: Follow the directions on page 5 to turn *The Elephant and the Monkey* patterns (pages 16–18) into visual props.

2. Scenery: For a puppet show, make a river from blue fabric and make trees from stacked blocks.

3. Bananas: Place self-stick Velcro® on the back of the bananas and the top of the tree. The fruit can then be detached and thrown down to the elephant.

4. Retell: Let the children manipulate the flannel board pieces or the puppets as you read the story. The children will also enjoy taking turns retelling the story all by themselves.

(fig. 4)? Go and pick some fruit for me and then you will find out which one of you is the best."

So the big elephant and the little monkey **stood up** and began their **walk** to the river. When they reached the river the little monkey said, "the water is too deep and I cannot swim."

The big elephant replied, "Hop on my back and I will carry you to the other side of the river." So, the little monkey **hopped** on the elephant's back, the elephant **stepped** into the water, and together they **swam** safely to the other side.

When the elephant and the little monkey reached the other side of the river, they **climbed** out of the water, and **looked up** at the tall fruit trees *(fig. 5)*. The fruit was at the top of the trees. How were they going to get the fruit down?

The big elephant **stretched** and **reached up with his trunk**, but his trunk was not long enough. Then the big elephant tried to **push** the tree down, but the tree was just too big.

The little monkey said, "I can **quickly climb** to the top of the tree and throw the fruit down for you to catch." The monkey **scampered up** the tree as fast as he could, **picked** the fruit *(fig. 6)*, and **threw** it down. The elephant **held up** his long trunk and **caught** the fruit as it fell.

The little monkey **climbed down** the tree and **back up** onto the big elephant's back. The little monkey **held** onto the fruit as the big elephant **swam** the two of them safely back across the river.

The big elephant and the little monkey **ran** over and **gave** the fruit to the wise owl. "Now wise owl, will you tell us which is the best? The elephant said, "**It is the best to be big and strong**!" The monkey said, "**It is the best to be little and fast.**"

The wise owl said to them, "You needed each other to get the fruit. It took the large size and strength of the big elephant to get across the river. It took the speed and climbing skills of the little monkey to get the fruit. I would say that both of you are the best!"   **THE END**

The Elephant and the Monkey Patterns

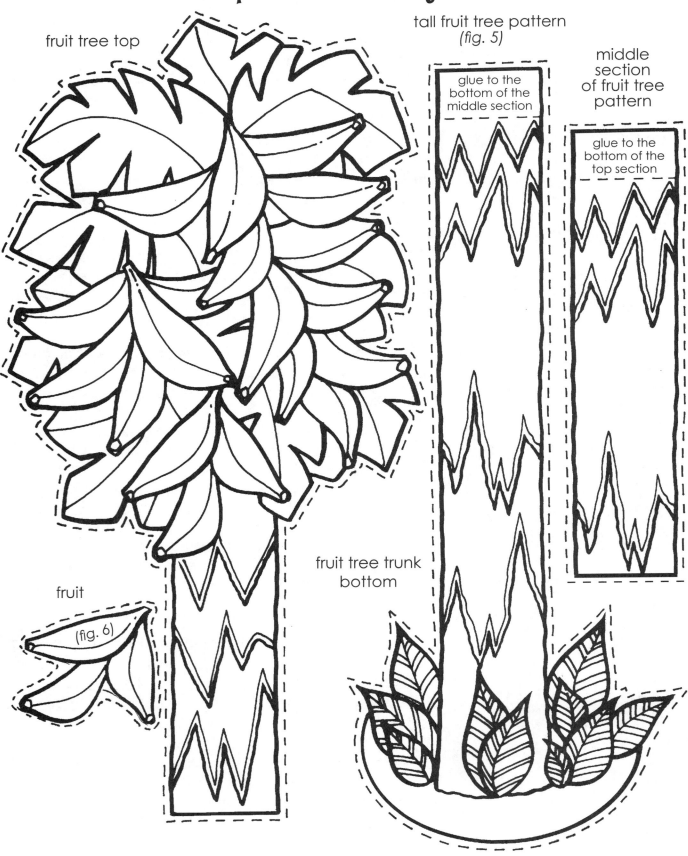

fruit tree top

tall fruit tree pattern
(fig. 5)

glue to the bottom of the middle section

middle section of fruit tree pattern

glue to the bottom of the top section

fruit

(fig. 6)

fruit tree trunk bottom

The Elephant and the Monkey Patterns

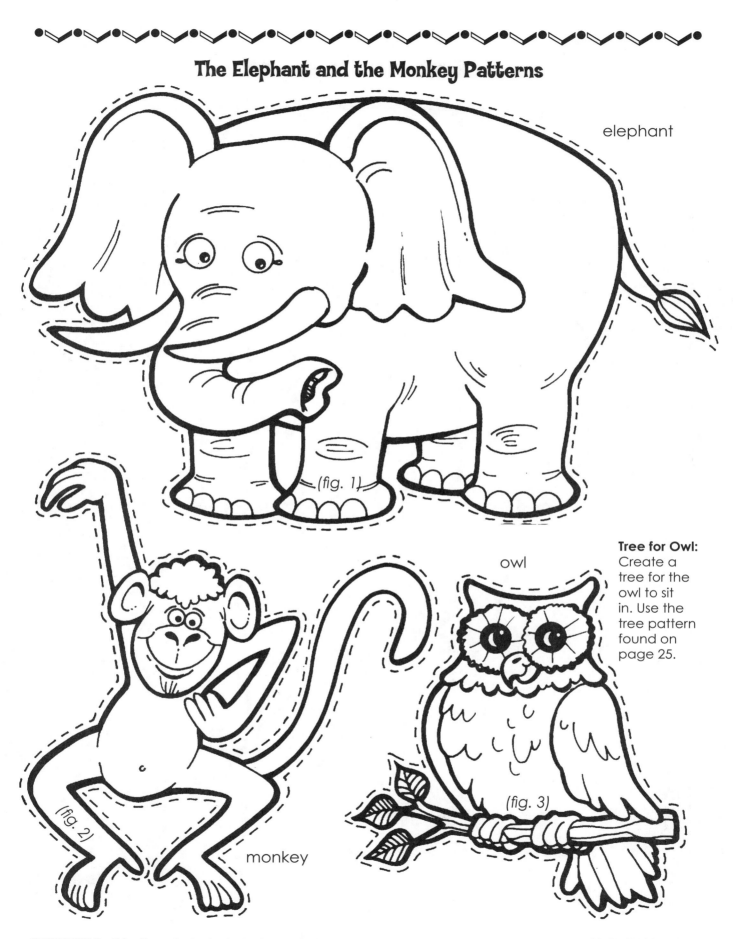

elephant

(fig. 1)

Tree for Owl: Create a tree for the owl to sit in. Use the tree pattern found on page 25.

owl

(fig. 2)

monkey

(fig. 3)

river and
fruit trees

(fig. 4)

The Mouse and the Thunder Storm

- unknown

This Story:

The Mouse and the Thunder Storm is an excellent story for helping children overcome a fear of thunder storms. It can also be used as a weather unit.

Basic Concepts:

1. Weather: Brainstorm a list of why we need rain and water and compile a list of weather words.

2. Vocabulary: Read the story in advance to identify the vocabulary that may be unfamiliar to your students. Some new words may be: **tremble**, **shiver**, **waddling**, and **scurried**.

Pantomime/Act-it-Out Story Directions:

1. Pantomime: Read the **bold-italized** action words slowly. This will help the children to listen and know when and what to pantomime. Have **all** the children pantomime the character of the little scared mouse.

2. Happy Chant: Teach the children the underlined sentences and have them repeat the sentences at the appropriate time during the story.

Flannel Board/Puppet Story Directions:

1. Visual Presentation: Follow the directions on page 5 to turn *The Mouse and the Thunder Storm* patterns (page 20) into visual props. Make a pond from blue paper and a green bush for the mouse to hide behind.

2. Retell: Let the children manipulate the flannel board pieces or the puppets as you read the story.

The Mouse and the Thunder Storm

Once upon a time, there was a little mouse *(fig. 1)* who was afraid of thunder storms. When she **heard** thunder in the sky she would **tremble** and **shake**. When she **saw** lightening in the sky she would **shake** and **shiver**. The other mice would tease her by yelling, "Thunder! Thunder! Thunder! Run and hide!" And the poor little mouse would always **run** and **hide**.

One sunny day, the little mouse went out for a long **walk**. She **walked** and **walked** and **walked**, when suddenly she realized that she was getting very thirsty. Just then some dark clouds *(fig. 2)* began to roll in, the thunder sounded, and it began to rain. The thunder storm **frightened** the little mouse and she began to **cry**. She **quickly ran** to find somewhere safe to **hide**.

From her hiding spot she **saw** a frog *(fig. 3)*. He was **hopping** and **dancing**. He loved the thunder storm! The frog cheered, " <u>**I am so happy. There will be water in the pond!**</u>"

Then the little mouse **saw** a duck *(fig. 4)*. The duck was **quacking** and **waddling**. She loved the thunder storm! The duck cheered, "<u>**I am so happy. There will be water in the pond!**</u>"

The little mouse said to herself, "They like thunder storms! Maybe thunder storms are good. From now on I will not be scared of thunder storms anymore!" Then she remembered how thirsty she was. The little mouse **scurried** down to the pond *(add paper pond)* and said, " <u>**I am so happy. There will be water in the pond!**</u>" And then she had a big drink of water! **THE END**

The Mouse and the Thunder Storm Patterns

duck

frog

(fig. 3)

mouse

(fig. 4)

(fig. 1)

gray thunder
cloud

(fig. 2)

Chicken Little

– a folk tale

This Story:

Chicken Little is a traditional folk tale. It can be enjoyed anytime, but it is especially fun during a thematic unit about the farm or farm animals.

Basic Concepts:

1. The Five Senses: Children Little **saw**, **heard**, and **felt** the sky falling. Could she have also **tasted** or **smelled** the sky? At the end of the story, let the children pretend they are Chicken Little and discover all the ways to **see**, **hear**, **feel**, **smell**, and **taste** an apple.

2. Vocabulary: Read the story in advance to identify the vocabulary that may be unfamiliar to your students. Some new words may be: **plop**, **scratching** and **terrible**.

3. The Animals' Names: Before you read the story, tell the children the names of all the animals. Can they identify the types of animals from their names?

Pantomime/Act-it-Out Story Directions:

1. Pantomime: Read the **bold-italized** action words slowly. This will help the children to listen and know when and what to pantomime. Let the children decide which animal's actions they would like to pantomime.

2. Individual story groups: Divide the children into story groups. They can take turns performing for each other.

Chicken Little

(Place the apple tree, fig. 8, on the board before beginning the story.)

Once upon a time there was a little chick named Chicken Little *(fig. 1)*. One day while she was **scratching** for food in the orchard, a little apple *(fig. 2)* fell – plop – right on top of her head! Chicken Little **jumped up** and squealed, "Oh, what was that? The sky is falling. I must go and tell the king."

And then she cried again!

> "Oh my goodness! The sky is falling!
> I saw it with my eyes. I heard it with my ears.
> And a piece of it fell right on top of my head."

Chicken Little **ran** and **bumped** right into Henny Penny *(fig. 3)*. "Why are you running?" asked Henny Penny.

Chicken Little cried!

> "Oh my goodness! The sky is falling!
> I saw it with my eyes. I heard it with my ears.
> And a piece of it fell right on top of my head."

"This is terrible," cried Henny Penny. "**Hurry** and **run**. We must go and tell the king."
Chicken Little and Henny Penny **ran** and **bumped** right into Cocky Locky *(fig. 4)*.
"Why are you running?" asked Cocky Locky.

Chicken Little cried!

> "Oh my goodness! The sky is falling!
> I saw it with my eyes. I heard it with my ears.
> And a piece of it fell right on top of my head."

"This is terrible," cried Cocky Locky. "**Hurry** and **run**. We must go and tell the king."
Chicken Little, Henny Penny, and Cocky Locky **ran** and **bumped** right into Ducky Lucky *(fig. 5)*.

3. Choral Chant: Have the children memorize, and then chant, the boxed three-line "sky is falling" exclamation. Add actions to make the chant even more dramatic. Here are some fun actions:

"Oh, my goodness! *(Raise arms and hands over head.)*

The sky is falling! *(Bring arms down and wiggle fingers.)*

I saw it with my eyes. *(Use both hands, and point to eyes.)*

I heard it with my ears. *(Both hands point to ears.)*

And a piece of it fell right on top of my head." *(On the word "head," children tap their own heads with both hands.)*

Flannel Board/Puppet Story Directions:

1. Visual Presentation: Follow the directions on page 5 to turn *the Chicken Little* patterns (pages 23–25) into visual props.

2. Feathers: All the story characters are birds. To add extra fun — glue craft feathers *(found at most craft stores)* on each of the birds.

3. Retell: Let the children manipulate the flannel board pieces or the puppets as you read the story. The children will also enjoy taking turns retelling the story all by themselves.

"Why are you running?" asked Ducky Lucky.

Chicken Little cried!

> **"Oh my goodness! The sky is falling!**
> **I saw it with my eyes. I heard it with my ears.**
> **And a piece of it fell right on top of my head."**

"This is terrible," cried Ducky Lucky. "**Hurry** and **run**. We must go and tell the king."

Chicken Little, Henny Penny, Cocky Locky, and Ducky Lucky **ran** and **bumped** right into Turkey Lurky *(fig. 6)*.

"Why are you running?" asked Turkey Lurky.

Chicken Little cried!

> **"Oh my goodness! The sky is falling!**
> **I saw it with my eyes. I heard it with my ears.**
> **And a piece of it fell right on top of my head."**

"This is terrible," cried Turkey Lurky. "**Hurry** and **run**. We must go and tell the king."

Chicken Little, Henny Penny, Cocky Locky, Ducky Lucky and Turkey Lurkey **ran** and **bumped** right into Hootie the Owl *(fig. 7 and 9)*.

"Why are you running?" asked Hootie the Owl.

Chicken Little cried!

> **"Oh my goodness! The sky is falling!**
> **I saw it with my eyes. I heard it with my ears.**
> **And a piece of it fell right on top of my head."**

"Are you sure the sky is falling?" asked Hootie the Owl. All at once, all the animals began to tell the tale of how the sky was falling and how a piece of the sky hit Chicken Little right on top of her head.

Chicken Little said, "I can prove it! I have a piece of the sky with me." And she **handed** Hootie the Owl what she was holding. Hootie **looked** at the piece of sky, he **smelled** the piece of sky, and then he actually **tasted** the piece of sky.

All the other animals **watched** and then realized that Chicken Little had been hit on the top of her head by an apple that had fallen from a tree. One by one all the animals **walked away**.

Hootie the Owl said to Chicken Little, "If you are a smart little chicken, you will eat this apple before your friends come back and want to eat it!" Feeling a little embarrassed, Chicken Little **ate** and **ate** and **ate**, until the apple was all gone! **THE END**

Chicken Little Patterns

apple

(fig. 2)

Chicken Little

(fig. 1)

Cocky Locky

(fig. 4)

Henny Penny

(fig. 3)

Chicken Little Patterns

Ducky Lucky

(fig. 5)

Hootie the Owl

(fig. 7)

(fig. 6)

Turkey Lurkey

Chicken Little Patterns

apple tree

Hootie's tree

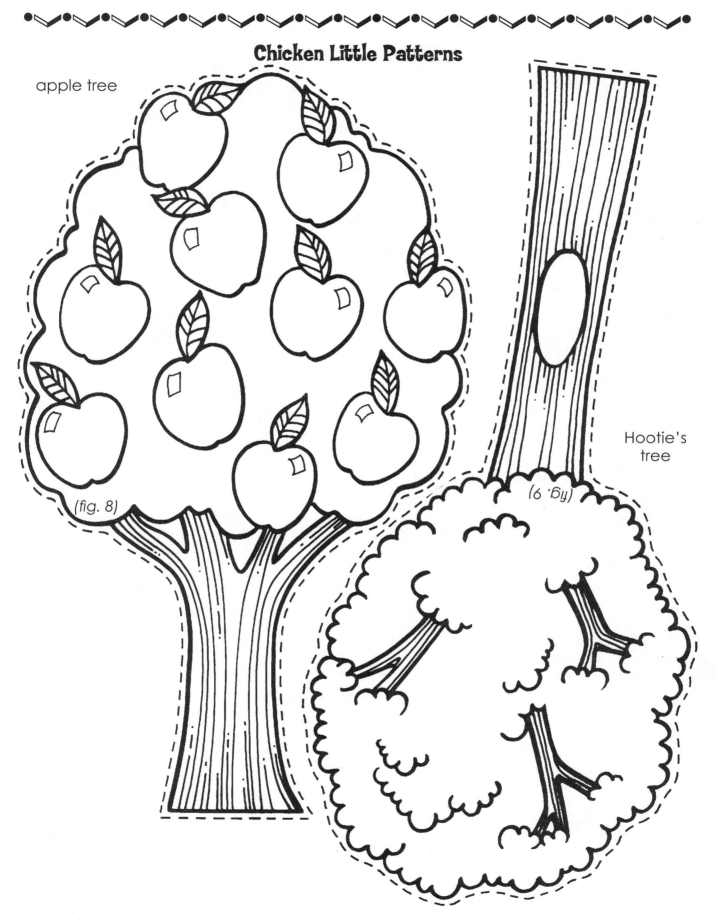

(fig. 8)

(fig. 9)

Why the Bear is Stumpty-Tailed

– a Norwegian tale

This Story:

Why the Bear is Stumpty-Tailed is a fun tale that can be used during thematic units on the seasons, forest animals, or can be enjoyed anytime.

Basic Concepts:

1. Real and Not Real Concepts: Before reading the story, show the children photographs of real bears and foxes. Discuss how a bear and a fox are the same and how they are different. After you have read the story, look at the photographs again.

2. Vocabulary: Read the story in advance to identify the vocabulary that may be unfamiliar to your students, such as: **horrified, tingling, stinging, bushiest, jealous, yank,** and **gigantic.**

Pantomime/Act-it-Out Story Directions:

1. Pantomime: Read the **bold-italized** action words slowly. This will help the children to listen and know when and what to pantomime. Divide the class in two—half pantomime the actions of the fox and the other half pantomime the actions of the bear.

2. Choral Chant: Teach the children the underlined phrase. Point or pause to provide a clue of when the children should recite the phrase.

Flannel Board/Puppet Story Directions:

1. Visual Presentation: Follow the directions on page 5 to turn *Why The Bear is Stumpty-Tailed* patterns (pages 28–30) into

Why the Bear is Stumpty-Tailed

(Place summer tree on board, fig. 1.) Once upon a time, many years ago, the bear *(fig. 4)* and the fox *(fig. 5)* both had tails that were long and bushy and beautiful. In truth, it was the bear who had *(pause)* **the longest and bushiest and most beautiful tail in the forest**, which made the fox very jealous.

One day, as the fox **hid** behind a bush, he **watched** the bear **walk** down to the lake. "I must think of a way to get rid of the bear's tail! I want to be the animal with *(pause)* **the longest and bushiest and most beautiful tail in the forest**," thought the fox.

The fox thought about the bear's beautiful tail all summer long. How could he get rid of the bear's tail? He wanted to be the animal with *(pause)* **the longest and bushiest and most beautiful tail in the forest**.

Before long the autumn winds began to blow. *(Place autumn tree on board, fig. 2.)* The leaves were turning to autumn colors of red, orange, and yellow. The fox still needed a plan. The bear's tail was still *(pause)* **the longest and bushiest and most beautiful tail in the forest**. The fox was becoming more and more jealous. He cried, "I want to be the animal who has *(pause)* **the longest and bushiest and most beautiful tail in the forest**."

The leaves on the trees were now beginning to fall to the ground, the winds were becoming colder, and snow was starting to fall. *(Place winter tree on board, fig. 3.)* Suddenly, an idea came to the fox. Earlier in the day he had seen a truck down by the lake and it was filled with fresh fish.

The fox chuckled, "Now I will have *(pause)* **the longest and bushiest and most beautiful tail in the forest**." The fox **ran** to the truck, **climbed** into the back, and **stole** a string of fish.

flannel board pieces or stick and string puppets.

2. Bush: Make a green construction paper bush for the fox to hide behind.

3. Velcro®: Attach self-stick Velcro® tabs to fig. 9 (bear) and fig. 10 (bear's tail) and to fig. 7 (string of fish) and to fig. 5 (fox) so the tail and the fish can be removed at the appropriate time during the story.

4. Retell: Let the children manipulate the flannel board pieces or the puppets as you read the story. The children will also enjoy taking turns retelling the story all by themselves.

Since it was winter, the fox knew that the bear had not had anything to eat in weeks and that he was **sound asleep** in his cave *(fig. 6)*. The fox, **swinging** the string of fish from his tail *(fig. 7)*, **walked back and forth** in front of the bear's cave. The bear **wiggled** and began to **wake up** when he **smelled** something fishy-good to eat. The fox chuckled again and thought, "Soon, I will have *(pause)* ***the longest and bushiest and most beautiful tail in the forest***."

The bear **wandered out** of his cave and asked the fox, "Where did you get those fish? The lake is frozen and we can't go fishing until spring."

"Oh bear!" replied the fox, "Come with me and I will show you how to fish in the winter." The bear agreed and together both animals **walked** down to the lake.

The fox kept thinking, "By tonight, I will have *(pause)* ***the longest and bushiest and most beautiful tail in the forest***."

When they reached the lake, the fox told the bear to cut a hole in the ice *(fig. 8)*. The bear, who was very strong, **cut a hole**. Then the fox explained to the bear *(use fig. 9 and fig 10)* that he should use his tail as a fishing pole and **stick it through the hole** and into the water.

The bear did as he was told and then asked, "Now that my tail is in the water, how will I catch the fish?"

"Oh," replied the fox, "Just wait and before long the fish will grab onto your tail." The fox quietly giggled and thought, "Soon, I will have *(pause)* ***the longest and bushiest and most beautiful tail in the forest***."

The bear **waited** and **waited** and **waited**. Suddenly, the bear realized that the water was turning to ice. "Help fox!" cried the bear, "What should I do? My tail is frozen in the water! It is tingling and stinging!"

The fox, pretending to **look concerned**, said, "Oh dear friend bear, don't worry. Your tail, *(pause)* ***the longest and bushiest and most beautiful tail in the forest***," is fine. The fish you have caught are making your tail tingle and sting. The bear was so excited because he believed that his tail was filled with delicious fish.

"How do I get the fish out of the ice?" questioned the bear.

The fox explained, " Pull your tail with one gigantic sideways yank. Your tail, *(pause)* ***the longest and bushiest and most beautiful tail in the forest***, will come out of the water and it will be covered with fish."

Well, the bear gave his tail **one gigantic yank**. But instead of the bear's tail coming out of the ice covered with fish — his poor tail **snapped** right off!" The bear who once had *(pause)* ***the longest and bushiest and most beautiful tail in the forest***," now had a short stumpty-tail!

The horrified bear **ran** the whole way back to his cave and **slept** all winter long!

The fox **giggled** and **laughed** and **shouted**, "Now I have *(pause)* ***the longest and bushiest and most beautiful tail in the forest***." And today, you will see that all of the bears in the forest have short stumpty-tails and all of the foxes have *(pause)* ***the longest and bushiest and most beautiful tails in the forest***." **THE END**

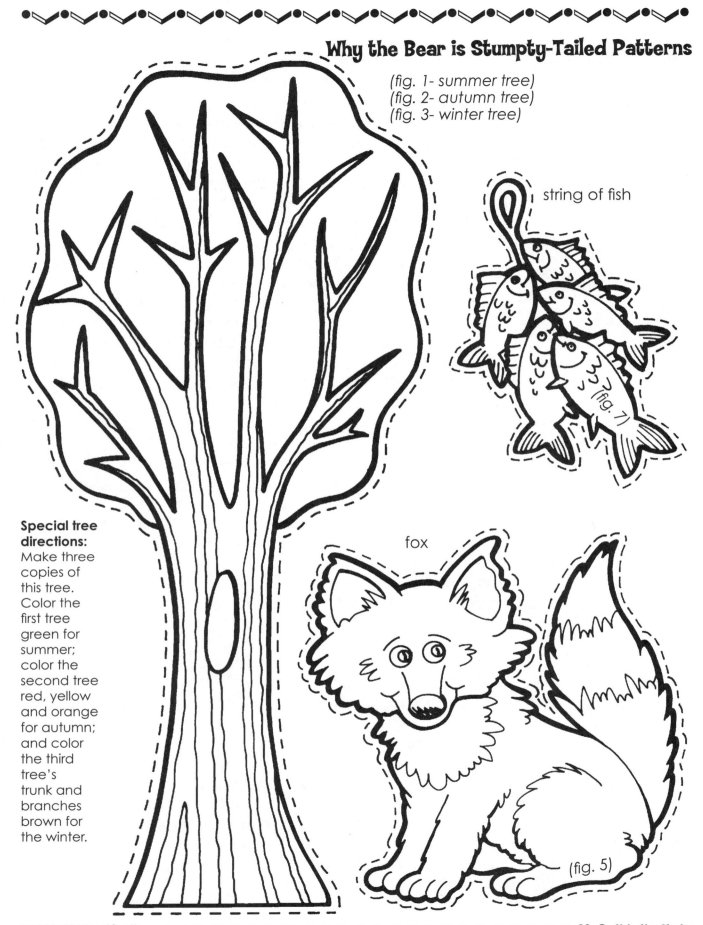

(fig. 1- summer tree)
(fig. 2- autumn tree)
(fig. 3- winter tree)

string of fish

(fig. 7)

Special tree directions:
Make three copies of this tree. Color the first tree green for summer; color the second tree red, yellow and orange for autumn; and color the third tree's trunk and branches brown for the winter.

fox

(fig. 5)

Why the Bear is Stumpty-Tailed Patterns

bear with long bushy tail

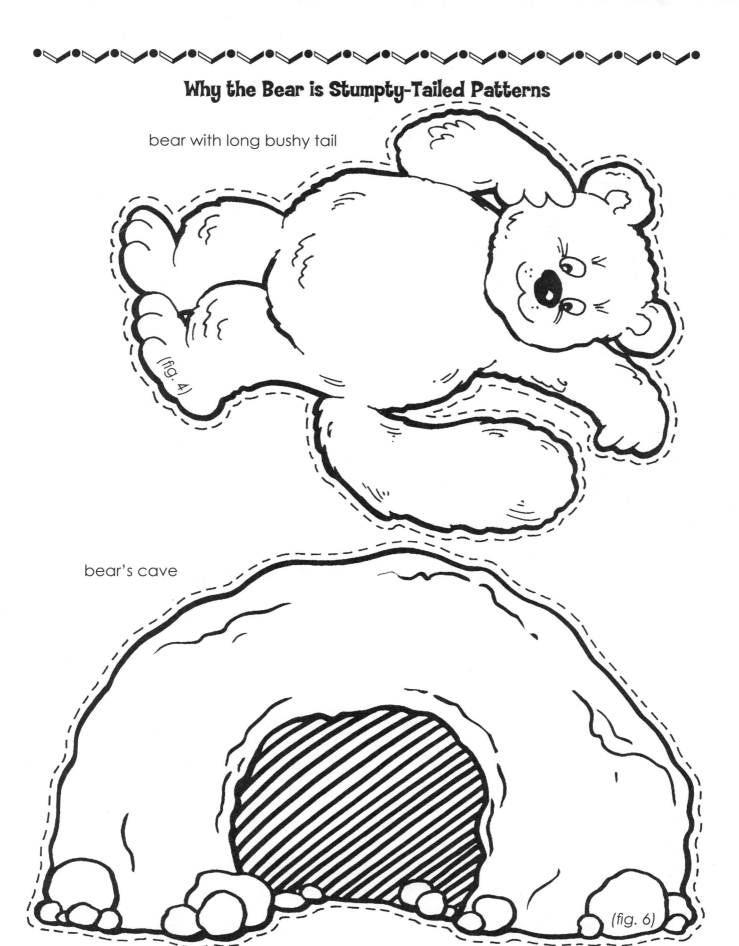

(fig. 4)

bear's cave

(fig. 6)

Why the Bear is Stumpty-Tailed Patterns

bear's bushy tail

bear with stumpty tail

frozen pond

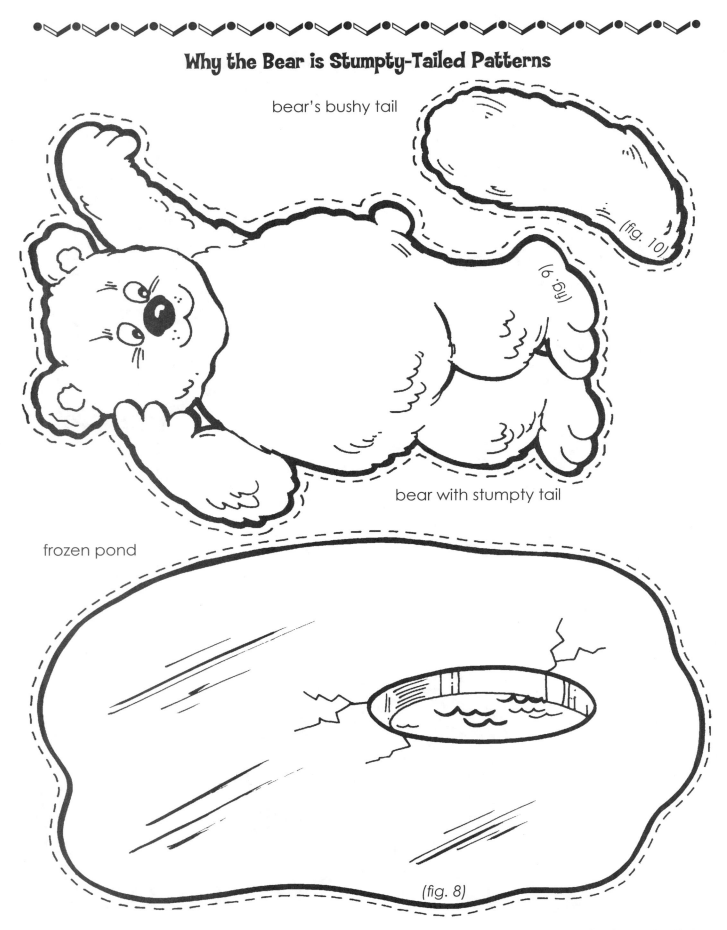

(fig. 10)

(fig. 9)

(fig. 8)

The Dog and the Bumble Bee

– a traditional tale

This Story:

This is a fun story that can be enjoyed anytime.

Basic Concepts:

1. Phonemic Awareness: Read the rhyme and ask the children to listen and identify all the words that rhyme with "**bee.**" Read again and listen for words that rhyme with "**oh.**" Read a third time and listen for words that rhyme with "**there.**"

2. Vocabulary: Read the story in advance to identify the vocabulary that may be unfamiliar to your students, such as: **replied**, **set out**, **adventuring**, and **yelped**.

Pantomime/Act-it-Out Story Directions:

1. Pantomime: Read the **bold-italized** action words slowly. Read the story twice. Each child should find a partner. One will pantomime the actions of the dog and the other will pantomime the actions of the bee—read again and have the children switch roles.

2. Memorize Chant: Have the children memorize the two-line boxed verse. Encourage them to say it dramatically.

Flannel Board/Puppet Story Directions:

1. Visual Presentation: Follow the directions on page 5 to turn *The Dog and The Bumble Bee* patterns (page 32) into flannel board pieces or stick and string puppets. The string puppets are very effective for this story. The bee can actually "fly" around the dog.

The Dog and the Bumble Bee

A little dog *(fig. 1)* **set out** one day, adventuring was he —
And what did he meet along the way
    But a great big bumble bee *(fig. 2)*!

(The children who are pretending to be the dog should walk around the room - the bees should suddenly jump in front of the dogs.)

> "Bzzz, bzzz, bzzz," said the bumble bee,
> "Little dog — stay away from me!"

(The bee buzzes around the dog.)

The little dog laughed,
Silly bee, you can't give me a scare.
I'm not afraid of you — and I'll bite you . . . there!

(Little dog pretends to laugh and then pretends to bite.)

> "Bzzz, bzzz, bzzz," said the bumble bee,
> "Little dog — stay away from me!"

(The bee buzzes around the dog.)

But the little dog *(fig. 3)* **opened** his mouth up wide —
    And just as you'd suppose—
"Very well," the bee replied — and **stung**
    The little dog's nose!

(Little dog opens mouth and bee pretends to sting the dog.)

The little dog *(fig. 4)* yelped, "Oh, oh, oh,"
    And the bee replied, "I told you so."
So the little dog turned — and **ran** did he —
    As fast as he could go —

(The little dog runs away and the bee shakes a finger at the fleeing dog.)

Now — NEVER AGAIN will he try to bite a bee!
    Absolutely NO!

THE END

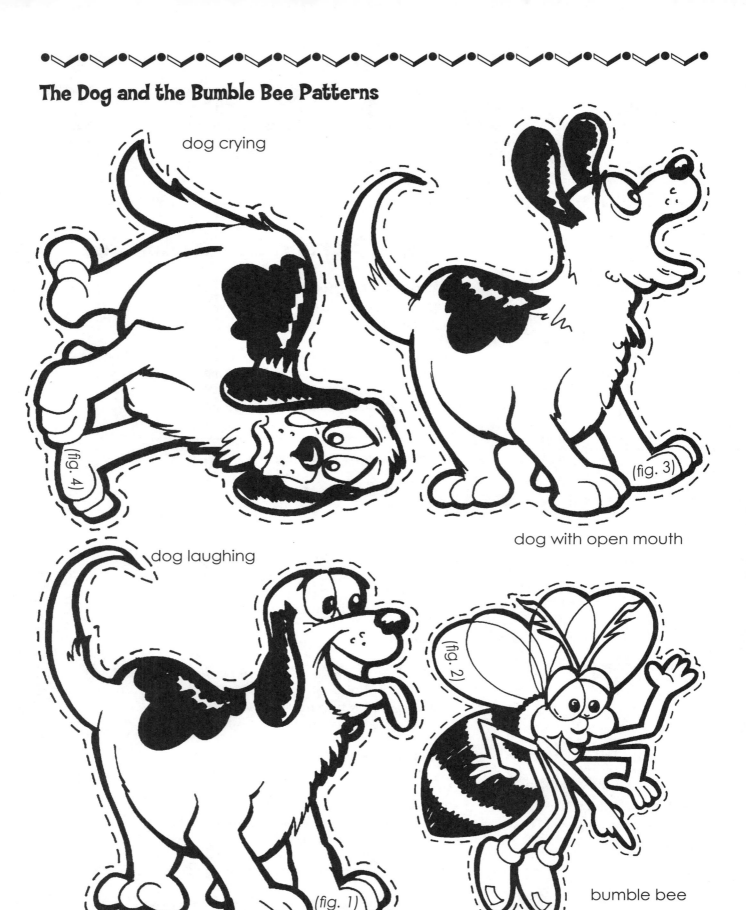

dog crying

(fig. 4)

dog with open mouth

(fig. 3)

dog laughing

(fig. 1)

(fig. 2)

bumble bee

The Town Mouse and the Country Mouse – a traditional tale

This Story:

The Town Mouse and the Country Mouse is a traditional tale that children love. It can also help children learn to appreciate what they have and not envy what others may have.

Basic Concepts:

1. Town and Country: Show the children various photographs of rural and urban living. Talk about the similarities and differences. Draw a large Venn diagram and cut and paste pictures for each section of the diagram.

2. Inference: After reading the story to the children, read the last paragraph again. What is the country mouse talking about when he says he doesn't like that kind of music?

3. Vocabulary: Read the story in advance to identify the vocabulary that may be unfamiliar to your students, such as: **enjoy**, **grumbled**, and **embarrassed**.

Pantomime/Act-it-Out Story Directions:

1. Pantomime: Read the **bold-italized** action words slowly. This will help the children to listen and know when and what to pantomime.

The Town Mouse and the Country Mouse

Once upon a time there was a sweet little country mouse *(fig. 1)*. He lived a simple life. He liked to **run** in the fields, **eat** corn and peas and bread *(fig. 3)*, and **sleep** in his old matchbox bed *(fig. 4)*.

One day the country mouse's cousin, the town mouse *(fig. 2)*, decided to visit his country cousin. The country mouse **ran** up to meet his town mouse cousin.

"Welcome town mouse. I am so glad that you came to visit the country." said the country mouse. "Tonight we will **eat** well. I have corn and peas and bread."

The two little mice **sat down** to **eat**. The town mouse **looked** at the food and said, "Is this all you have to **eat** cousin?" Where is the cheese? Where is the cream? Where is the ice cream?"

The country mouse, feeling a little embarrassed, replied, "This is what I **eat** everyday. This food is healthy and it is easy to find in the country." The town mouse **ate** the food but he did not enjoy it.

Evening came and it was time to go to **sleep**. The country mouse said, "I am happy to share my matchbox bed with you cousin."

The town mouse grumbled and said, "I cannot **sleep** in a matchbox and I need to **eat** better food. I cannot stay in the country any longer. I am going back to town. Cousin, if you ever come to town you can **eat** <u>the very best</u> food and you can **sleep** in <u>the very best</u> bed. Good-bye!"

The town mouse began **walking** back to town, leaving the country mouse **sitting** alone and **looking very sad**.

The next day the country mouse thought, "Maybe I

2. Words "Eat" and "Sleep":
Every time the children hear the words "**ate** and **eat**" they should pantomime eating with a spoon. Every time they hear the words "**sleep, slept,** or **sleeping**" they should put their hands against their cheek, and pretend to sleep.

2. "...the very best..." Teach the children the underlined phrase and have them recite it during the story.

Flannel Board/Puppet Story Directions:

1. Visual Presentations:
Follow the directions on page 5 to turn The *Town Mouse and the Country Mouse* patterns (pages 34–36) into flannel board pieces or stick and string puppets.

2. Scenery: Have a puppet show. Make string puppets. Build a real matchbox bed and a cotton ball bed for the two mice. Attach a triangle stand on the back of each table so that they can actually stand up.

3. Retell: Let the children manipulate the flannel board pieces or the puppets as you read the story.

should go to town? I would like to **eat** <u>the very best</u> food and I would like to **sleep** in <u>the very best</u> bed."

So the country mouse **packed** his bags and began **walking** to town. He finally reached the home of his town mouse cousin. He **knocked** on the door. The town mouse **opened** the door and **clapped** his hands with joy when he saw his country cousin.

"**Come in**! **Sit down**. It is almost time for dinner," said the town mouse. "Now you will get to **eat** <u>the very best</u> food *(fig. 5)*." The two mice **ate** cheese and cream and ice cream. The country mouse thought, "My cousin was right. This is <u>the very best</u> food."

When evening came, the two mice **crawled** on top of <u>the very best</u> bed the country mouse had ever seen. The country mouse **wiggled** and thought, "This is <u>the very best</u> bed I have ever **slept** on."

Suddenly, they heard some loud growling *(fig. 7)*. The country mouse **shook** with fear. The town mouse **sat up** and said, "Don't worry, it's just the two large dogs that live in this house. They always growl."

The country mouse **jumped out** of bed, **packed** his bags, and said to the town mouse, "I am going home. I think that I have <u>the very best</u> food to eat, and that my matchbox is <u>the very best</u> bed! And I really do not think that is <u>the very best</u> music for a mouse!" The country mouse **ran** home as fast as he could.   **THE END**

The Town Mouse and the Country Mouse Patterns

(fig. 7)

The Town Mouse and the Country Mouse Patterns

country
mouse

(fig. 1)

town
mouse

(fig. 2)

country
mouse's bed

REDMATCH

(fig. 4)

The Town Mouse and the Country Mouse Patterns

town mouse's
dinner table

country mouse's
dinner table

(fig. 3)

(fig. 5)

town mouse's
bed

(fig. 6)

Myrtle, the Turtle, and the Leprechaun – unknown

Myrtle, the Turtle, and the Leprechaun

This Story:

Myrtle, the Turtle, and the Leprechaun is a fun story to tell during the month of March when you are discussing St. Patrick's Day.

Basic Concepts:

1. Slow and Fast Concepts: Discuss the concepts of **slow** and **fast**. Play some music. When the music is soft, the children should dance very slow – just like Myrtle. When the music is loud, the children should dance very fast–just like the leprechaun would move.

2. Real and Pretend: Leprechauns are pretend characters. Research some leprechaun legends and share them with your class.

3. Vocabulary: Read the story in advance to identify the vocabulary that may be unfamiliar to your students, such as: **plopped, nodded, scruffy, creeping, spotted, leprechaun,** and **temperamental**. Have the children practice pantomiming these actions before you read the story.

4. If you had a wish . . .: Ask the children if they had been Myrtle, and the leprechaun wanted to grant them a wish, what would they wish for? If they could make a wish for someone else - who would get the wish and what would that wish be?

Once upon a time there was a very **slow-moving** turtle, named Myrtle *(fig. 1)*. Myrtle was a happy turtle who was content **creeping along** the road. She liked taking her time getting from one place to another.

One day, as she was **crawling slowly,** she **spotted** a **quick movement** behind a large group of brightly colored flowers *(fig. 2)*.

"Who is there?" Myrtle asked in a slow voice.

"No one is here." said the small voice.

Myrtle **smiled** a slow smile and said, "Oh, please come out. I would not hurt you."

A very tiny man *(fig. 3)* **jumped out** from behind the flowers. He was dressed all in green, had a scruffy little beard, and wore a bright green top hat.

Myrtle **slowly nodded her head** at the little man and said, "Hello, Mr. Leprechaun."

The Leprechaun **looked surprised** and asked, "How do you know who I am?"

Myrtle **chuckled** and said, "Oh, Mr. Leprechaun, anyone who saw you would know who you are. There are not many tiny bearded men dressed all in green. Why are you so far away from home?"

The Leprechaun **sat down** on the grass, **frowned,** and said, "I wanted to take a little trip, but now I suppose you'll be wantin' me pot of gold."

Myrtle **looked surprised** and said, "Why would I want your gold?"

She **slowly shook her head** and said, "I have no need for your gold."

The Leprechaun **stood up** and **stamped his foot**. Leprechaun's are known for being temperamental. "Well

Pantomime/Act-it-Out Story Directions:

1. Pantomime: Read the bold-italized action words slowly. This will help the children to listen and know when and what to pantomime.

2. Extra Fun Ways to Read: The teacher should read Myrtle's sentences slowly and deliberately. Read the leprechaun's sentences very fast. This will also help the children to better understand how to move while pantomiming the story as well as gaining a better understanding of the character's personalities.

Flannel Board/Puppet Story Directions:

1. Visual Presentation: Follow the directions on page 5 to turn *Myrtle, the Turtle, and the Leprechaun* patterns (pages 39–40) into flannel board pieces or stick and string puppets.

2. Myrtle's Gold Wings: Place a piece of self-stick Velcro® on Myrtle's back and the corresponding piece on the wings. They can be "attached" and then "unattached" during the story.

3. Extra Scenery: Add a yellow felt sun and a couple of white felt or cotton batting clouds as an extra touch for a flannel board presentation.

4. Retell: Let the children manipulate the flannel board pieces or the puppets as you read the story. The children will also enjoy taking turns retelling the story all by themselves.

then," he said, "I suppose you'll be wantin' me to grant you a wish."

Myrtle very **slowly** started to **crawl away**. "No thank you Mr. Leprechaun. There is nothing that I want or need."

The Leprechaun **jumped up and down** and then **plopped down** on the ground. "If you are not takin' me gold, then you must let me grant you a wish."

Myrtle **slowly turned around** and said, "Very well. I would like to give my friend Delia Duck some ribbons for her birthday."

The Leprechaun **waved both of his arms over his head** and said, "poof!" Myrtle thanked the Leprechaun and once again **slowly started crawling** home.

"Stop!" yelled the Leprechaun as he **spun around in a circle**. "I must grant you a wish for yourself. It's a rule of the Leprechauns! There must be something that you want. Maybe you would you like to swim like a fish?"

Myrtle **laughed** and said, "I already know how to swim."

"How about a coat of feathers just like your friend Delia Duck?" asked the Leprechaun.

Myrtle **giggled**, "Oh no, I like my shell."

"Myrtle, you move so slowly. Maybe you would like wings so you could fly through the sky with great speed?" asked the Leprechaun as he **pretended to fly**.

Myrtle **sat right up** when she heard this idea. "Maybe it would be fun to move faster than I do now? All right Mr.. Leprechaun, I wish I had a beautiful pair of gold wings," wished Myrtle.

The Leprechaun **waved both of his arms over his head** and said, "poof!" Beautiful gold wings *(fig. 4)* appeared on the back of Myrtle's shell. At first she began to **slowly flap her wings**. Then she **flapped faster and faster** until Myrtle was **flying** through the sky. She **swooped up and then down**. She **flew faster and faster**.

Myrtle **flew** right past a very shocked looking Sammy Sparrow *(fig. 5)*. Sammy heard Myrtle screaming, "Help me Sammy! I do not know how to land!"

Sammy **flew** beside Myrtle and **helped** her **land safely** on the ground.

"Well now Myrtle, did you have a fun flight?" asked the Leprechaun.

"I did not!" replied Myrtle. "I do not like to fly!"

The poor Leprechaun **sat down**, put his **hands on his face**, and **shook his head.** "Granting a wish is suppose to make you happy," sighed the Leprechaun.

Myrtle was a smart turtle. "Mr. Leprechaun, I wish my gold wings would disappear! That would make me happy."

The Leprechaun **waved both of his arms over his head** and said, "poof!"

The Leprechaun disappeared and so did the gold wings on Myrtle's shell.

As Myrtle began her **slow crawl** back home she **spotted** a lovely ribbon *(fig. 6)* laying in the road. Next to the ribbon was a card. Myrtle **picked up** and **read** the card, "Happy Birthday to Delia Duck, from your good friend, Myrtle, the Turtle. "What a thoughtful Leprechaun," thought Myrtle.   **THE END**

Myrtle,
the Turtle

**Myrtle, the Turtle,
and the Leprechaun
Patterns**

(fig. 1)

row of flowers
(make 2)

(fig. 2)

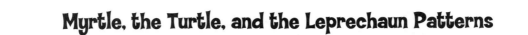

Myrtle, the Turtle, and the Leprechaun Patterns

Leprechaun

Sammy Sparrow

(fig. 5)

(fig. 3)

ribbon and
birthday
card

Happy Birthday
to Delia Duck
From
your friend,
Myrtle, the Turtle

(fig. 6)

(fig. 4)

gold wings

The Bee and the Goats

– a folk tale

The Bee and the Goats

This Story:

The Bee and the Goats is a fun story to tell and has many repetitive lines.

Basic Concepts:

1. Up and Down and In and Out Concepts: Discuss the concepts of **up** and **down** and **in** and **out**. On the flannel board, use the goats, hill, and turnip field patterns to demonstrate up, down, in and out.

2. Vocabulary: Read the story in advance to identify the vocabulary that may be unfamiliar to your students, such as: **whimpered, whined, moaned, groaned,** and **calico.**

3. Inference: *Question 1:* The story does not tell us why the goats ran into the turnip field and refused to leave. Why do you think the goats wanted to be in the turnip field and not on the grassy hill?
Question 2: Why do you think the little boy says, "If they run into the turnip field tomorrow, I will pat their backs and make a buzzing sound."?

Pantomime/Act-it-Out Story Directions:

1. Pantomime: Read the **bold-italized** action words slowly. This will help the children to listen and know when and what to pantomime.

2. Dramatic Noises: The boy and each of the animals have a special sound they make: the boy **whimpered**, the calico cat **whined**, the

Once upon a time there was a little boy *(fig. 1)* who lived with his mother, father, and three goats. One goat was very big *(fig. 2)*. One goat was very little *(fig. 3)*. And one goat was not so big and not so little *(fig. 4)*.

Not far from the boy's house was a grassy hill *(fig. 5)*. Every morning the boy would **run** with the goats up to the top of the small hill. He would **watch** them all day long as they **ate** the good green grass. Then in the evening the boy and the goats would **run** back down the hill.

One morning, the little boy began **running** up the hill, but the goats did not follow. The three goats **ran away** from the boy and **ran** right into the turnip field *(fig. 10)*.

The little boy **waved** his arms, he **called** for the goats, he **jumped up and down**, but no matter what he did the goats would not leave the turnip field.

The little boy did not know what to do, so he **sat** down at the bottom of the hill and **cried** and **cried** and **cried**.

Before long, a calico cat *(fig. 6)* **walked** up to the boy and asked him, "Why are you **crying**?"

The boy **whimpered**, "I am **crying** because my goats are in the turnip field and I cannot get them out."

The cat **smiled** and said, "Oh, I can get them out of the turnip field."

The calico cat **ran** and **ran** and **ran** around the goats, but the goats would still not leave the turnip field.

So, the calico cat **sat down** by the boy and together they **cried** and **cried** and **cried**.

Before long, a shaggy dog *(fig. 7)* **walked** up to the boy and the calico cat and asked, "Why are you two **crying**?"

The boy **whimpered** and the cat **whined**, "We are **crying** because the goats are in the turnip field and we cannot get them out."

shaggy dog **moaned**, the masked raccoon **groaned,** and the bee **buzzed**. Assign each child a character and have them practice the above sounds. Then read the story and have the children make the appropriate sound instead of reading the actual underlined word.

2. Crying: Have the children rub their eyes each time they hear the circled words **cried** or **crying**.

Flannel Board/Puppet Story Directions:

1. Visual Presentation: Follow the directions on page 5 to turn *The Bee and the Goats* patterns (pages 43–46) into flannel board pieces or stick or string puppets.

2. Retell: Let the children manipulate the flannel board pieces or the puppets as you read the story again.

Extra Fun: Tell the story again and have the children keep the story going by adding more helpful animals.

The shaggy dog **smiled** and said, "Oh, I can get them out of the turnip field."

The shaggy dog **ran** and **ran** and **ran** around the goats, but the goats would still not leave the turnip field.

So, the shaggy dog **sat down** by the boy and the calico cat and together they (cried) and (cried) and (cried.)

Before long, a masked raccoon *(fig. 8)* **walked** up to the boy, the calico cat, and the shaggy dog and asked, "Why are you three (crying)?"

The boy **whimpered**, the calico cat **whined**, and the shaggy dog **moaned**, "We are (crying) because the goats are in the turnip field and we cannot get them out."

The masked raccoon **smiled** and said, "Oh, I can get them out of the turnip field."

The masked raccoon **ran** and **ran** and **ran** around the goats, but the goats would still not leave the turnip field.

So, the masked raccoon **sat down** by the boy and the calico cat and the shaggy dog and together they (cried) and (cried) and (cried.)

Before long, a **buzzing** bee **flew** by the boy, the calico cat, the shaggy dog, and the masked raccoon and asked, "Why are you four (crying)?"

The boy **whimpered**, the calico cat **whined**, the shaggy dog **moaned**, and the masked raccoon **groaned**, "We are (crying) because the goats are in the turnip field and we cannot get them out."

The **buzzing** bee **smiled** and said, "Oh, I can get them out of the turnip field."

The boy and the animals asked, "How can you do that. Not one of us could get the goats to leave the turnip field and we are all much bigger than you."

"Just watch," said the bee.

The **buzzing** bee **flew** and **flew** and **flew** around the goats. Then he **sat** on the back of the very big goat. The very big goat was **scared** and **ran** out of the turnip field. Then the bee **flew** over and **sat** on the back of the very little goat. The very little goat was **scared** and **ran** out of the turnip field.

Finally, the **buzzing** bee **flew** over and **sat** on the back of the goat who was not so big and not so little. The goat who was not so big and not so little was **scared** and **ran** out of the turnip field.

The boy, the calico cat, the shaggy dog, and the masked raccoon all **watched** the **buzzing** bee. Suddenly, the little boy **stood up** and **ran** after his goats. He yelled back at his new friends, "I had better follow my goats home. If they run into the turnip field tomorrow, I will pat their backs and make a **buzzing** sound!"

All the animals **laughed**.

THE END

The Bee and the Goats Patterns

(fig. 3)

fig. 9

bee

very little goat

(fig. 4)

the goat who was not so very big and not so very little

(fig. 2)

very big goat

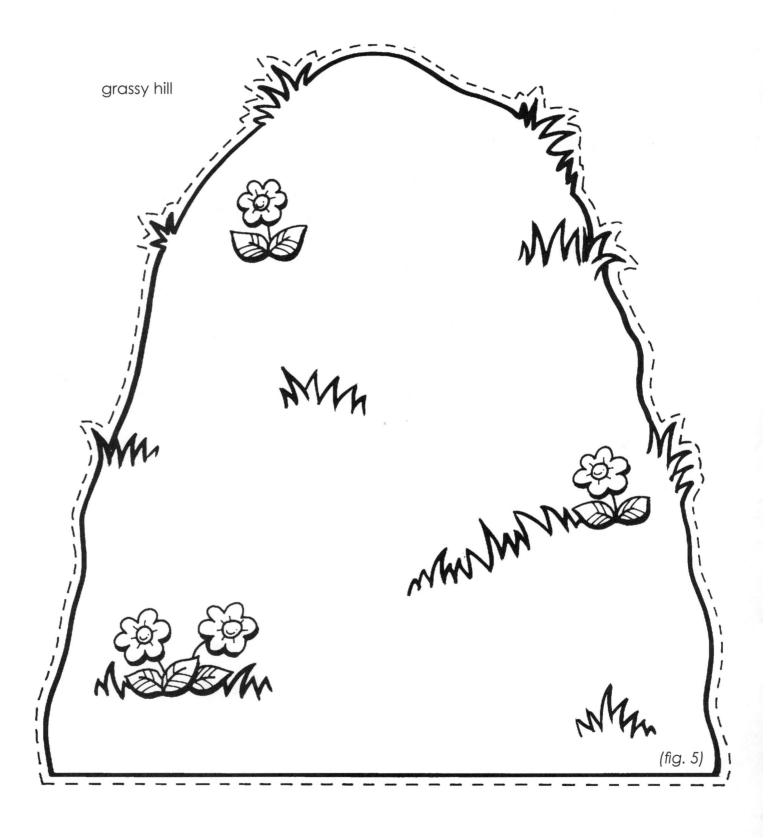

grassy hill

(fig. 5)

The Bee and the Goats Patterns

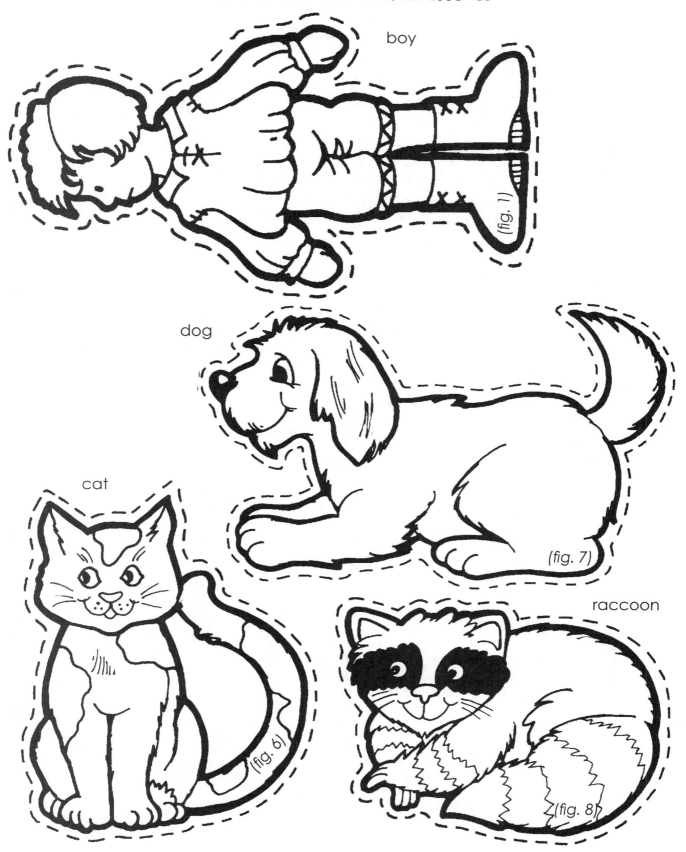

boy

(fig. 1)

dog

(fig. 7)

cat

(fig. 6)

raccoon

(fig. 8)

The Bee and the Goats Patterns

turnip field

(fig. 10)

The Bear Cub's Adventure

– a rhyming tale

This Story:

The Bear Cub's Adventure is a fun story to use anytime.

Basic Concepts:

1. Phonemic Awareness/ Rhyming Words: Read the words below and have the children identify the ones that rhyme in each line:

tree / see / owl
held / bear / there
side / with / cried
tight / might / smell

2. Vocabulary: Read the story in advance to identify the vocabulary that may be unfamiliar to your students, such as: **rude** and **stretching**.

3. Surprise Ending: Pause before you read the line, "Just a mean old owl." Ask the kids to guess what is in the tree.

Pantomime/Act-it-Out Story Directions:

1. Pantomime: Read the **bold-italized** action words slowly. This will help the children to listen and know when and what to pantomime.

Flannel Board/Puppet Story Directions:

1. Visual Presentation: Follow the directions on page 5 to turn *The Bear Cub's Adventure* patterns (page 48) into flannel board pieces or stick and string puppets.

Extra Touch: Place self-stick Velcro® on the tree hole and on the back of the owl. The owl can then be added and removed as appropriate.

2. Stuffed Animals: This is a fun story to retell using a teddy bear and a large card stock tree.

The Bear Cub's Adventure

(place tree, fig. 1 on flannel board and bear cub, fig. 2 at the bottom of the tree)

Once I **saw** a bear cub,	*(hands at side)*
Looking up at a hole in a tree!	*(point up)*
What was he **thinking**?	*(touch head)*
And what did he **see**?	*(point to eyes)*

With his nose **held up** high,	*(hold nose up)*
He **sniffed** here and there.	*(pretend to sniff)*
What did he **smell**?	*(hands-up, questioning)*
Was there honey up there?	*(point up)*

(move the bear cub, fig. 2 up the tree as if he was climbing)

He **stretched** out his arms,	*(stretch arms out)*
And **held** onto the tree.	*(pretend to grab tree)*
He **climbed** up the trunk.	*(pretend to climb tree)*
So he could better **see**.	*(pretend to look around)*

Holding on very tight,	*(pretend to hold tight)*
Up **climbed** the bear.	*(pretend to keep climbing)*
Grabbing with all his might,	*(keep climbing tree)*
He was almost there!	*(keep climbing tree)*

(move bear cub, fig. 2 and have him pretend to put his arm in the hole)

Finally he was near the hole,	
And he **put** his paw inside.	*(pretend to put paw in)*
"Ow" he loudly **growled**,	*(everyone growl)*
Jumped down and then he cried!	*(pretend to jump down and cry)*

(jump bear cub, fig. 2 down to the ground)

There wasn't any honey.	*(shake head "no")*
There wasn't any food.	*(again, shake head "no")*
Just a mean old owl.	*(hands around eyes - to look like an owl)*

(place owl, fig. 3 on the tree hole)

Who was very, very rude!	*(fold arms across chest - look perturbed)*

The Bear Cub's Adventure

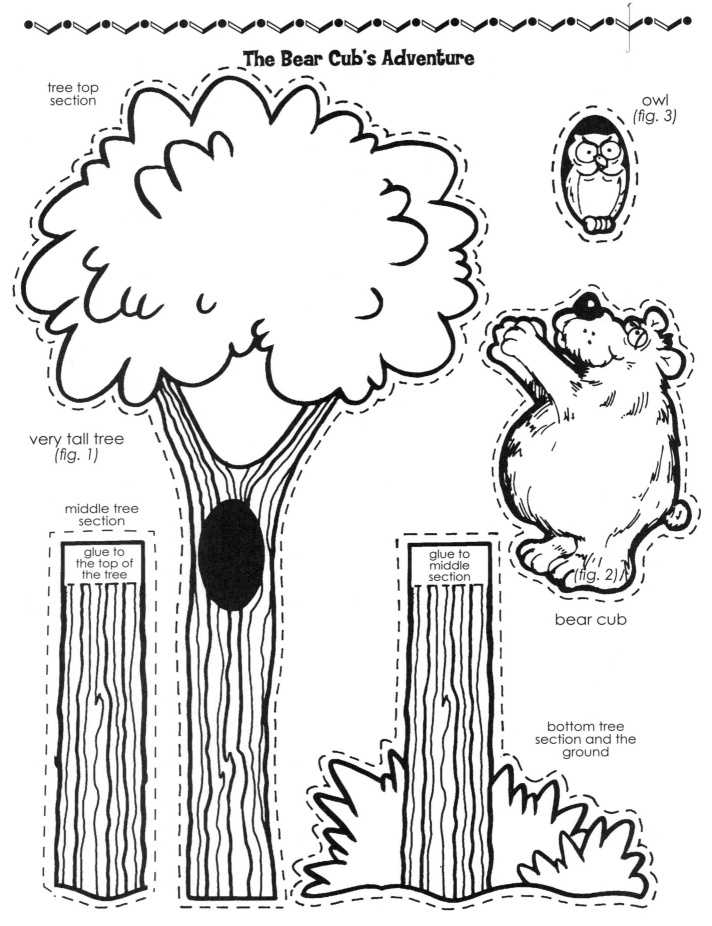

tree top section

owl
(fig. 3)

very tall tree
(fig. 1)

middle tree section

glue to the top of the tree

glue to middle section

(fig. 2)

bear cub

bottom tree section and the ground

Why the Cedar is Ever Green

- a folk tale

Why the Cedar is Ever Green

This Story:

Why the Cedar is Ever Green is a delightful story to tell when autumn is approaching. You can discuss how leaves change color, why birds fly south, and why the animals are busy collecting food. It is also a story that can be enjoyed anytime.

Basic Concepts:

1. Autumn: Discuss the changing seasons with the children. Show them photographs of trees during the different seasons. Collect leaves and sort them according to shape and color.

2. Migration: In the story Why the Cedar is Ever Green, the little bird is left behind when the flock flies south for the winter. Research with the class the various kinds of birds that fly south from a northern climate and then identify those birds that remain in the north all winter.

Have your class make pinecone bird feeders. Provide each child with a small pinecone. Cover the pinecone in peanut butter or lard (be aware of food allergies before bringing anything with peanuts into the classroom) and then roll the pinecone in birdseed. Attach a string for hanging.

3. Vocabulary: Read the story in advance to identify the vocabulary that may be unfamiliar to your students, such as: **shelter**, **shivered**,

This story begins in the North Forest when the beautiful days of summer were gone. Most of the green leaves on the trees *(place figures 1, 2, 3, and 4 on the flannel board)* had turned bright shades of red, orange, and yellow. The branches of the trees **danced** and **swayed** as the North Wind *(fig. 6)* began to **blow** his chilly music, and the squirrels **scampered** to **collect** nuts for the long winter days ahead.

It was a bright autumn day. The birds began to **gather** in flocks *(fig. 5)*. Soon they would fly south where they would stay until spring came back to the North Forest again. When the birds were ready the leader shouted to the flock, "We are all here! Let's go! Up, up, and away **they all flew**!" *(move fig. 5 to the top corner of the flannel board)*

But alas! The youngest bird *(fig. 7)*, who was so excited for his first journey south did not go with the flock. When the leader yelled, "Up, up, and away!" The little bird **flapped his wings** too hard, **flew** too low, and **crashed** into an old oak tree and **broke** his wing.

The poor little bird **cried** as he **watched** the rest of the flock fly out of sight *(remove fig. 5)*. The little bird **shivered** and said, "What shall I do? I cannot fly with a broken wing! Winter is coming and I shall freeze! I need to find a warm shelter."

The little bird **hobbled** around the North Forest **dragging** his broken wing. He **stopped** by the old oak tree *(fig. 1)* and asked, "Excuse me, Mr. Oak tree, my wing is broken and I cannot fly south. May I find shelter in your branches?"

But the oak tree *(move fig. 1 as if dancing)* was having such a merry time **dancing** and **swaying** to the music of the North Wind that he did not hear the little bird.

scampered, **gather**, **hobbled**, **collect**, **heal**, and **snuggled**. Have the children practice pantomiming these actions before you read the story.

4. Forever Green: Copy page 52 for each child. Have them color the cedar tree green and draw a picture of the little bird nestled somewhere on its branches.

Pantomime/Act-it-Out Story Directions:

1. Pantomime: Read the **bold-italized** action words slowly. This will help the children to listen and know when and what to pantomime.

2. Retelling through a Performance: Divide the class into groups of six children. Let each child have a role that they wish to play: little bird, oak tree, maple tree, elm tree, cedar tree, or Jack Frost. Let the children practice dramatizing this tale. After some practice, let them perform the story for the other groups or for another classroom.

Flannel Board/Puppet Story Directions:

1. Visual Presentation: Follow the directions on page 5 to turn the *Why the Cedar Tree is Ever Green* patterns (pages 51–54) into flannel board pieces and stick and string puppets.

2. Retell: Let the children manipulate the flannel board pieces or the puppets as you read the story.

So, the little bird **hobbled** around the North Forest **dragging** his broken wing. He **stopped** by the old maple tree *(fig. 3)* and asked, "Excuse me, Mr. Maple tree, my wing is broken and I cannot fly south. May I find shelter in your branches?"

But the maple tree *(move fig. 3 as if dancing)* was having such a merry time **dancing** and **swaying** to the music of the North Wind that he did not hear the little bird.

So, the little bird **hobbled** around the North Forest **dragging** his broken wing. He **stopped** by the old elm tree *(fig. 2)* and asked, "Excuse me, Mr. Elm tree, my wing is broken and I cannot fly south. May I find shelter in your branches?"

But the elm tree *(move fig. 2 as if dancing)* was having such a merry time **dancing** and **swaying** to the music of the North Wind that he did not hear the little bird.

"Oh, dear! Oh, dear! Without a warm shelter I shall freeze," cried the little bird.

Just then the little bird heard someone call to him, "Little bird, come to me and I will give you shelter," said the cedar tree *(fig. 4)*. "My soft thick branches will keep you safe and warm."

The little bird **hobbled** over to the cedar tree **dragging** his broken wing. The gentle tree **picked him up** and **placed** the little bird safely on a branch. The little bird **snuggled** into the branches. This was the perfect place for him to heal. The little bird should be able to fly by springtime.

That night, Jack Frost *(fig. 8)* came back into the North Forest. He had not finished painting all the trees with the autumn colors of red, orange, and yellow.

"Oh no!" said Jack Frost, "there is a cedar tree that is still green. I must **paint** it an autumn color."

Shaking his branches, the cedar tree said, "Please Jack Frost, "let me keep my warm green needles a little longer. I am protecting this little bird who has a broken wing."

Jack Frost **smiled** and said to the cedar tree, "You may keep your green color forever. You will be the only trees in the forest that will be forever green and it is because you were so kind and loving to this little bird.

And to this day, the cedar tree and all the trees of its family, keep their warm beautiful green color throughout the winter—while all the other trees stand bare.   **THE END**

oak tree

elm tree

cedar tree
(fig. 4)

Why the Cedar is Ever Green Patterns

little bird

(fig. 7)

Jack Frost

maple tree

(fig. 3)

(fig. 8)

flock of birds

North Wind

(fig. 5)

(fig. 6)

Nightmare Go Away!

– a rhyming tale

This Story:

This is a fun story that is just a little bit scary, which makes it fun to use during the month of October. It is also a story that can help children overcome their fear of nightmares.

Basic Concepts:

1. What scares you?: Have the children discuss things that scare them: spiders, the dark, etc. How do they overcome their fears? Who helps them feel better?

2. Vocabulary: Read the story in advance to identify the vocabulary that may be unfamiliar to your students, such as: **shivering** and **howling**. Have the children practice pantomiming these actions before you read the story.

Pantomime/Act-it-Out Story Directions:

1. Pantomime: Read the **bold-italized** action words slowly. This will help the children to listen and know when and what to pantomime.

2. Class Performance: Divide the class into 7 groups. Each group memorizes a verse.

Flannel Board/Puppet Story Directions:

1. Visual Presentation: Follow the directions on page 6 to turn *Nightmare Go Away!* patterns (pages 56–59) into flannel board pieces or stick and string puppets.

2. Retell: Let the children manipulate the flannel board pieces or the puppets as you read the story.

Nightmare Go Away!

Verse 1
There's a nightmare in my closet,
That makes me **shake** and **shiver**.
I want him to just go away.
I want to send him up the river!

(Before reading the story, place fig. 1, the nightmare, behind fig. 2, the closet door. Add fig. 5 window, fig. 4 bed, and fig. 3 the boy pointing to the door. Read verse 1 and remove fig. 3)

Verse 2
I should plan what I will do,
If he **opens** that closet door.
I'll **wrap him** in brown paper,
And I'll sell him at the store.

(Add fig. 6, read verse 2, and then remove fig. 6.)

Verse 3
If he **opens** that closet door,
In the middle of the night.
I'll **jump up** and yell "**boo**!"
I'll give that nightmare a fright!

(Add fig. 7, read verse 3, and then remove fig. 7.)

Verse 4
If that nightmare starts howling,
And tries to scare me.
I'll **pick him up** and **throw** him,
And he'll land in a tree.

(Add fig. 8, read verse 4, and then remove fig. 8.)

Verse 5
But now I **hear** some crying.
Coming from behind that closet door.
Is that nightmare scared of me?
Or is it something more?

(Move fig. 3 near the closet door, read verse 5, and then remove fig. 3.)

Verse 6
I **tip-toed** to the closet,
And **opened** the door up wide.
There sat a **shivering** nightmare,
Hiding behind the clothes inside.

(Add fig. 9 tip-toe boy, read verse 6, and open the closet door during the second line of the verse. Remove fig. 9)

Verse 7
Well, I **held** out my hand,
And said, Will you be my friend?"
Out **stepped** the nightmare,
And he gave me a **hug** – The End!

(Add fig. 3, read verse 7, and then have the boy and nightmare hug.)

Nightmare Go Away! Patterns

the nightmare
(fig. 1)

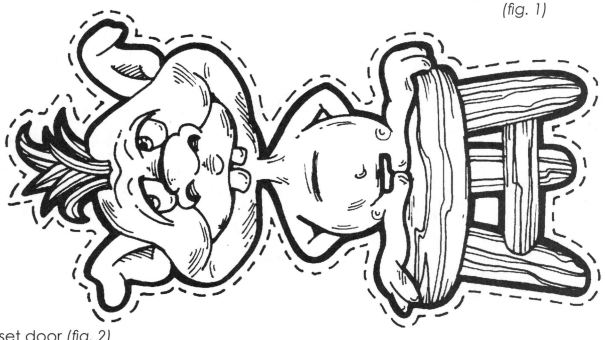

closet door *(fig. 2)*

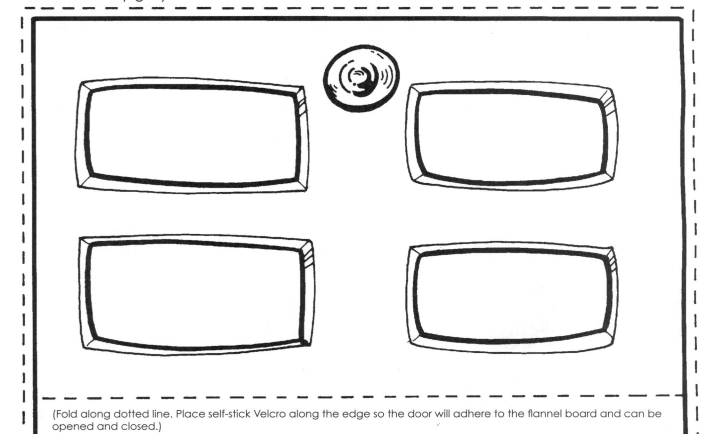

(Fold along dotted line. Place self-stick Velcro along the edge so the door will adhere to the flannel board and can be opened and closed.)

Verse 2 (fig. 6)

Verse 3 (fig. 7)

Verse 4 *(fig. 8)*

boy on tip toes *(fig. 9)*

boy pointing *(fig. 3)*

(fig. 5)

window in boy's bedroom

(fig. 4)

boy's bed

The Turtle and the Eagle

– an Aesop fable

This Story:

The Turtle and the Eagle is an old Aesop fable that helps children realize to be careful about what they wish for!

Basic Concepts:

1. Predict: The turtle promises the eagle a treasure from the sea. He never says what the treasure is. Brainstorm with the children what they think the turtle was going to give the eagle.

2. Vocabulary: Read the story in advance to identify the vocabulary that may be unfamiliar to your students, such as: **pleaded**, **hovered**, **soared**, and **swooped**.

Pantomime/Act-it-Out Story Directions:

1. Pantomime: Read the **bold-italized** action words slowly. This will help the children to listen and know when and what to pantomime.

Flannel Board/Puppet Story Directions:

1. Visual Presentation: Follow the directions on page 5 to turn *The Turtle and the Eagle* patterns (page 61) into flannel board pieces or stick and string puppets.
Velcro®: Place self-stick Velcro® on the back of fig. 3 (scared turtle) and on the talons on fig. 2 (eagle) so the turtle can be carried.

2. Retell: Let the children manipulate the flannel board pieces or the puppets as you read the story.

The Turtle and the Eagle

Once upon a time there was a turtle *(fig. 1)* who **crawled very slowly**. It took such a long time to get anywhere. He would **slowly lift one leg** and then he would **slowly lift the other leg**. As hard as the turtle tried, he could not move any faster.

One day when the turtle was **sitting** in the sun, he noticed how fast all the birds could fly. The birds would **flap their wings** and then **soar** through the sky. **Up and down** they **flew**. **Flying fast** and then **flying slow**.

The turtle **slowly lifted up his head** and called to his friend the eagle *(fig. 2)*, "Friend eagle! You are the fastest flier of all the birds! If you will come down here and teach me how to fly, I will give you a treasure found in the sea."

The eagle **swooped down**, **hovered over** the turtle, and said, "Turtle, that would be impossible. You were never meant to fly because you do not have any wings."

The turtle **slowly stood up** and pleaded for the eagle to teach him how to fly.

The eagle finally agreed to try. He **grabbed** the turtle's shell *(fig 2. grabs onto fig. 3)*, **flapped his wings**, and took off **flying**.

The poor turtle was so **frightened**. He **closed his eyes** and **shook** with fear.

"Eagle, listen to me," cried the turtle, "I have learned my lesson. I was not meant to fly. Please put me back on the ground!"

As the eagle **soared**, he replied, "Did you ask me to put you down'?"

The turtle **nodded** and yelled, "yes!"

So, from far above the trees the eagle let go and **dropped** the turtle. Luckily, the turtle landed with a huge splash in the middle of the pond.

The turtle *(fig. 1)* was glad to be down and was happy that he was not hurt. He **swam very fast** to the edge of the pond. The turtle then realized, "I can **move fast** when I am in the water. "

THE END

The Turtle and the Eagle Patterns

eagle

(fig. 2)

scared turtle

turtle looking brave

(fig. 3)

(fig. 1)

Little Red Shoes

– traditional

Little Red Shoes

This Story:

Little Red Shoes is a charming story about being needed. The shoes need someone to wear them and they found the perfect person.

Basic Concepts:

1. Big and Little Concepts: Discuss the concepts of **big** and **little**. Provide objects (or shoes) and have the children order them according to largest to smallest or smallest to largest.

2. Vocabulary: Read the story in advance to identify the vocabulary that may be unfamiliar to your students, such as: **nodded**, **pitter-patter**, and **cobbler**.

Discuss that a cobbler makes shoes. Let the children pretend to be cobblers and design and draw a pair of shoes. Display them on a bulletin board. To make this extra fun, have the children design shoes that the duck, cat, and squirrel could have worn.

Pantomime/Act-it-Out Story Directions:

1. Pantomime: Read the *bold-italized* action words slowly. This will help the children to listen and know when and what to pantomime.

2. Say "pitter-patter": Another fun addition is to teach the children the underlined phrase. Explain that each time you point your finger or raise your hand the children should say the phrase out loud and drum their hands on their legs.

(place fig. 1 on left side of flannel board) Once upon a time there was an old cobbler. He made a little pair of bright shiny red shoes. Most people do not have such small feet, so consequently no one was interested in buying the little red shoes.

The little red shoes **sat** on the cobbler's shelf for so long that they were sad and now covered in dust.

"This is no fun," said one little red shoe, "I think we should run away."

The other little red shoe **nodded** in agreement. The two little red shoes *(fig. 2 & 3)* **jumped** off the shelf and out the door they **ran**—**pitter-patter**, **pitter-patter**, **pitter-patter**.

"Stop!" yelled a squirrel *(fig. 4)*, "I want to wear you." The squirrel **jumped** into the little red shoes and **ran around**. "Now, climb that tree," she said.

"But we cannot climb," said the little red shoes.

"Then I cannot wear you," said the squirrel. The squirrel **kicked off** the little red shoes and away they **ran**—**pitter-patter**, **pitter-patter**, **pitter-patter**.

"Stop!" yelled a duck *(fig. 5)*, "I want to wear you." The duck **jumped** into the little red shoes and **ran around**.

"Now, swim in the pond," she said.

"But we cannot swim," said the little red shoes.

"Then I cannot wear you," said the duck. The duck **kicked off** the little red shoes and away they **ran**—**pitter-patter**, **pitter-patter**, **pitter-patter**.

"Stop!" yelled a cat *(fig. 6)*, "I want to wear you." The cat **jumped** into the little red shoes and **ran around**.

"Now, run," she said.

"But there are only two of us and you have four feet," said the little red shoes.

"Then I cannot wear you," said the cat. The cat **kicked off** the little red shoes and away they **ran**—**pitter-patter**, **pitter-patter**, **pitter-patter**.

Flannel Board/Puppet Story Directions:

1. Visual Presentation: Follow the directions on page 5 to turn *The Little Red Shoes* patterns (pages 63–64) into flannel board pieces or stick and string puppets.

2. Add-on Characters: this is a great story for adding-on to. After reading about the squirrel, the duck, and the cat, ask the children to add more animals who want to wear the shoes. Remember, they must also come up with a reason why each animal really cannot wear them.

The little red shoes **ran** and then **stopped** when they spotted a little girl *(fig. 7)*. She was **standing** all alone. She was **crying** and she was barefoot.

The little red shoes said to the little girl, "Will you wear us? We are the perfect size. We can keep your feet warm and we can **run**!" Then the shoes **ran around in circles** to show the little girl how fast they were—**_pitter-patter_**, **_pitter-patter_**, **_pitter-patter_**.

The little girl *(fig. 8)* **put on** the little red shoes. Her feet were warm, her heart was happy, and she **ran all around** the town showing off her new little red shoes—**_pitter-patter_**, **_pitter-patter_**, **_pitter-patter_**.

THE END

Little Red Shoes Patterns

shoes on store shelf

(fig. 1)

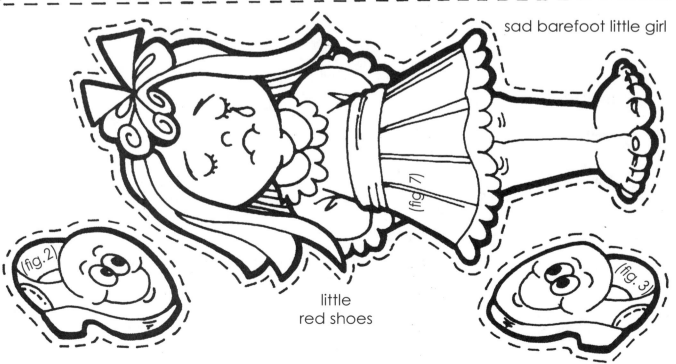

sad barefoot little girl

(fig. 7)

little red shoes

(fig. 2)

(fig. 3)

Little Red Shoes Patterns

happy girl
with red shoes
on her feet

squirrel wearing
red shoes

(fig. 8)

(fig. 4)

duck
wearing
red shoes

(fig. 5)

(fig. 6)

cat
wearing
red shoes